THE HISTORIAN'S CONTRIBUTION TO
ANGLO-AMERICAN MISUNDERSTANDING

THE HISTORIAN'S CONTRIBUTION TO ANGLO-AMERICAN MISUNDERSTANDING

Report of a Committee on National Bias in Anglo-American History Textbooks

by
RAY ALLEN BILLINGTON
With the collaboration of
C. P. HILL, ANGUS J. JOHNSTON II,
C. L. MOWAT and CHARLES F. MULLETT

Hobbs, Dorman & Company, Inc. — Publishers
NEW YORK   BUENOS AIRES

Library of Congress Card Number 66-17595

HD

74 354

First Published in 1966
Routledge & Kegan Paul Limited
Broadway House, 68-74 Carter Lane
London, E.C. 4

Printed in the United States of America

CONTENTS

v

Contents

vi

ILLUSTRATIONS

PREFACE

THIS book can trace its origins to a seminar on 'Perspectives on the American Revolutionary Era' which in the autumn of 1960 brought together at Colonial Williamsburg a group of scholars from England, the United States, and Canada. Two of those scholars, Professor Harry C. Allen of University College, University of London, and Professor Richard P. McCormick of Rutgers University, fell to discussing national bias in the secondary school textbooks of their respective nations. This casual conversation, as often happens, was destined to mushroom into a full-scale investigation, complete with professional and foundation support, and conducted by a hierarchy of committees.

The first step was to secure the backing of the three professional associations most concerned: the Historical Association of England and Wales, the British Association for American Studies, and the American Historical Association. Dr. Boyd Shafer, executive secretary of the latter society, was first approached, and gave the project his enthusiastic support. Under his guidance a detailed plan was prepared for submission to the three associations during the winter of 1960–1961. In November the Historical Association of England and Wales endorsed this plan; the council of the American Historical Association took similar action in December. The officials of these societies, together with those of the British Association for American Studies, undertook the additional responsibility of soliciting funds necessary to conduct the investigation. These were obtained in the spring of 1962 through the generosity of the Nuffield Trust of England and the Ford Foundation of the United States.

Next came the drafting of the usual committees. A Sponsoring Committee was named first, composed of Professor G. R. Potter of the University of Sheffield, Professor Reginald

F. Treharne of the University College of Wales, Aberystwyth, and Mr. E. H. Dance of Wolverhampton representing the Historical Association of England and Wales; Professor Harry C. Allen of University College, London, representing the British Association for American Studies; and Professors Caroline Robbins of Bryn Mawr College, Richard P. McCormick of Rutgers University, and Ray A. Billington of Northwestern University, representing the American Historical Association. This committee defined the principal lines of inquiry and established the methods that would be used in textbook analysis.

Its principal task was to select a Working Party that would carry on the investigation and prepare a publishable report. This was named during the autumn of 1962: Professor C. L. Mowat of the University College of North Wales, Bangor, Mr. C. P. Hill of the Department of Education, University of Exeter, Dr. Angus J. Johnston II of the Social Studies Department, New Trier High School, Winnetka, Illinois, and Dr. Ray A. Billington, now of the Henry E. Huntington Library, chairman. Dr. Boyd C. Shafer of the American Historical Association and Professor Richard P. McCormick of Rutgers University agreed to co-operate closely with the Working Party.

Procedures were then agreed upon. Two possible methods of textbook analysis could be employed. One would encourage each member of the Working Party to read widely and with little guidance, isolating instances of nationalistic bias whenever detected. The other would direct the analysis to specific historical episodes which seemed especially susceptible to biased treatment, with each member of the Working Party following agreed-upon techniques in identifying these instances. The latter method seemed to promise better results. It would allow analysis in depth, and would highlight the contrasting views of national bias held by British and American analysts. Hence the Planning Committee agreed that the Working Party should concentrate on three episodes: (1) the American Revolution, (2) the War of 1812, and (3) the First World War. It was also agreed that members of the Working Party should define nationalistic bias in terms suggested by Mr. E. H. Dance in a helpful memorandum prepared for the committee, and in that same author's study of the subject: *History the Betrayer: a Study of Bias* (Hutchinson, London, 1960). A bibliography prepared by Mr. Dance also allowed members of the Working Party to sample representative modern works dealing with national bias in historical studies.

The next step was to select textbooks for analysis. Thanks largely to the help of a member of the Working Party, Mr. C. P. Hill, himself a textbook author of note well acquainted with the English educational system, the choosing of English books presented no great problem; Mr. Hill after consultation with other teachers provided the committee with a list of books most widely used in both Grammar Schools and Secondary Modern Schools at the 12 to 16 age level. Selection of the textbooks most popular in American Junior High Schools and High Schools proved more difficult; publishers were unwilling to reveal sales statistics while state adoption lists varied too widely to be useful. Eventually the Working Party sought the advice of three experts in the field of secondary school history teaching: Professors Erling Hunt of Columbia University, William H. Cartwright of Duke University, and Richard E. Gross of Stanford University. Each generously supplied a list of textbooks that he considered most popular; insomuch as these lists agreed in almost every detail it was possible to distil from them a selection of the textbooks that provide nearly all of the instruction in American history in Junior and Senior High Schools in the United States.

Following these procedures, the Working Party determined to analyse the following books:

A. AMERICAN JUNIOR HIGH SCHOOL

Mabel B. Casner and Ralph H. Gabriel, *Story of the American Nation* (Harcourt, Brace & World, New York, 1962).

Gertrude Hartman, *America Land of Freedom* (D. C. Heath, Boston, 1961).

Edna McGuire and Thomas B. Portwood, *Our Free Nation* (The Macmillan Company, New York, 1961).

I. James Quillen and Edward Krug, *Living in Our America* (Scott, Foresman, Chicago, 1961).

Howard B. Wilder, Robert P. Ludlum and Harriett McCune Brown, *This Is America's Story* (Houghton Mifflin, Boston, 1963).

Preface

B. AMERICAN SENIOR HIGH SCHOOL

John R. Alden and Alice Magenis, *A History of the United States* (American Book Company, New York, 1962).

Henry W. Bragdon and Samuel P. McCutchen, *History of a Free People* (The Macmillan Company, New York, 1964).

Leon H. Canfield and Howard B. Wilder, *The Making of Modern America* (Houghton Mifflin, Boston, 1962).

Ruth Wood Gavian and William A. Hamm, *United States History* (D. C. Heath, Boston, 1960).

Henry F. Graff and John A. Krout, *The Adventure of the American People* (Rand McNally, Chicago, 1961).

David S. Muzzey and Arthur S. Link, *Our American Republic* (Ginn, Boston, 1963).

Lewis Paul Todd and Merle Curti, *Rise of the American Nation* (Harcourt, Brace & World, New York, 1961).

Clarence L. Ver Steeg, *The American People Their History* (Row Peterson, Evanston, Illinois, 1962).

Fremont P. Wirth, *United States History* (American Book Company, New York, 1961).

C. ENGLISH GRAMMAR AND SECONDARY MODERN SCHOOLS

C. J. Acheson, *The New Age* (G. Bell, London, 1961).

M. E. Beggs-Humphreys and D. W. Humphreys, *Everyday History. Book Two: The World Changes, 1688–1830* (George Philip, London, 1961).

C. H. C. Blount, *History through the Ages, Second Series Book 5: The Last Hundred Years* (Oxford University Press, Oxford, 1956).

S. Reed Brett, *From George III to George VI. A Brief History of Britain from 1760 to 1952* (Edward Arnold, London, 1959).

Constance M. Broadway, *Building the Empire* (Oxford University Press, Oxford, 1951).

E. H. Carter and R. A. F. Mears, *A History of Britain* (Oxford University Press, Oxford, 1960).

H. A. Clement, *The Story of Britain* (George G. Harrap, London, 1958).

E. H. Dance, *British and Foreign History. Book Two: New Europe and the New World. Book Three: The Modern World* (Longmans, London, 1957).

Kingston Derry, *British History from 1760 to 1945* (G. Bell, London, 1960).

C. B. Firth, *Road to Modern Europe, 1789–1945* (Ginn, London, 1949).

S. E. Gunn, *Journey Through History. Book IV: A World of Nations* (Edward Arnold, London, 1956).

C. P. Hill, *A History of the United States* (Edward Arnold, London, 1961).

L. F. Hobley, *Britain's Place in the World* (Oliver & Boyd, Edinburgh, 1960).

R. I. James, *The United States* (Ginn, London, 1951).

Donald Lindsay and E. S. Washington, *A Portrait of Britain from Peril to Pre-eminence, 1688–1851* and *A Portrait of Britain between the Exhibitions, 1851–1951* (Oxford University Press, Oxford, 1952 and 1954).

H. C. Knapp-Fisher, *Everyday History. Book Four: The World Today* (George Philip, London, 1958).

Patrick Larkin, *England Old and New* and *Crown, People and Commonwealth* (John Murray, London, 1954 and 1960).

Sir Henry Marten and E. H. Carter, *Histories. Book Four: The Modern Age* (Basil Blackwell, Oxford, 1961).

Elsa Nunn, *History, Second Series. Book One: The Growth of the British Commonwealth* (Ginn, London, 1949).

George W. Southgate, *A Textbook of Modern English History. Book Two: The Hanoverian Period and After, 1714–1960* (J. M. Dent, London, 1959).

I. Tenen, *This England* (Macmillan, London, 1962).

R. J. Unstead, *England. Book 3: The Rise of Great Britain, 1688–1837* and *Book 4: A Century of Change, 1837–Today* (A. & C. Black, London, 1963).

E. Wynn Williams, *The Kingsway Histories. Book Three: George I to Waterloo* and *Book Four: Modern Britain and the World* (Evans Brothers, London, 1959).

Geoffrey Williams, *Portrait of World History. Book II: Reformation to Revolution* (Edward Arnold, London, 1962).

Certain features should be noted about these histories. Most important is the subject matter. As one would expect, the United States books deal with American history, the British books with British history, except for two textbooks on American history written and published in England. No American high school textbook in British history has been analysed since, except in rare instances, the subject is no longer taught in American high schools. Examination of a textbook in world history widely used in the United States showed that the space allotted to the events under analysis was too negligible to permit meaningful appraisal.

The variation in subject-matter between British and American textbooks posed problems that could never be completely resolved. American textbooks cover a relatively brief time span; their authors therefore can devote a relatively large number of pages to the Revolution, the War of 1812, and the First World War. British texts, on the contrary, must tell the story of a thousand years of history and, with the respect for tradition that still governs in England, must pay proper attention to the earlier years. Their authors are correspondingly cramped for space in treating modern events, to the extent that such a minor episode in Britain's history as the War of 1812 can warrant but scant attention, and even the First World War appears slighted by American standards. A comparison of such differing works is always unfair to one or the other, and usually to the volume that is more compressed.

Despite these handicaps, the Working Party feels that its analysis techniques have proved effective in revealing the extent of nationalistic bias present in today's textbooks. The method employed in this analysis will make this clear. The appropriate passages in each of the textbooks were read by all members of the Working Party. Each member then prepared an extensive report, listing and classifying every exhibition of bias that was noted. These initial reports were discussed at a meeting of the Working Party held in Washington, D.C. in the summer of 1963; the conclusions reached in this exchange were then employed in a further analysis that went on through the next year. Reports based on this study were submitted to the chairman in May, 1964, and incorporated in a preliminary draft of this final report. This, in turn, was thoroughly discussed at a meeting of the Working Party held in London during the summer of 1964. There, certain conclusions, now incorporated in the final chapter of this book, were agreed upon.

In presenting its report, the Working Party has felt it best to omit specific identification of each passage cited to typify nationalistic bias. These references will be revealed to anyone sufficiently concerned to correspond with the chairman, who has retained a footnoted copy of the report. The committee's purpose is not to condemn any author, for all are guilty of national bias in one form or another. Rather it is hoped that the revelation of bias in the better and most popular textbooks used in the schools of England and the United States will make authors, publishers, and teachers aware of the necessity for careful scrutiny of every word and every sentiment, in order to guard against those unconscious prejudices that have marred international understanding in the past.

I

THE FORMS OF
NATIONALISTIC BIAS

EXTBOOK writers of today can seldom be charged with the
sins of their nineteenth-century predecessors who deliberately distorted the truth to magnify the virtues of their
national heroes and discredit their nation's enemies.[1] Gone is
the time when a writer could tell his young readers (as did
Jacob Abbott in his 1856 *Narrative of Universal History*) that 'it
is not possible for the imagination to conceive of characters
more selfish, profligate, and vile, than the line of English
kings'. We have happily outgrown the day when George III
was pictured to the young American as a tyrant bent on crush-
ing democracy under an iron heel, when the defeat of the
British at New Orleans was made understandable to high
school readers as divine retribution for the burning of Washington, or when Lloyd George was depicted as a crafty scoundrel
determined to defeat the godlike Woodrow Wilson's plans for
a just peace. Evidences of overt bias such as these have largely
disappeared. No one is likely to say of future statesmen what
was once said of Franklin D. Roosevelt: that he adopted an
anti-British policy in the last months of World War II because
he had read the wrong textbooks.

[1] Most of the concepts and many of the examples used in this chapter have
been shamelessly borrowed from E. H. Dance, *History the Betrayer. A Study in Bias*
(1960). The literature on national bias in textbooks is relatively extensive. Among
the most useful of these are: A. C. F. Beales, *Memorandum on Nationalism in the
Teaching of History* (1939); E. H. Dance, *History Without Bias?* (1954); J. A.
Lauwery, *History Textbooks and International Understanding* (1951); *A Study of
National History Textbooks Used in the Schools of Canada and the United States* (1947);
H. Vigander, *Mutual Revision of History Textbooks in Nordic Countries* (1950); and
The Teaching of History and International Understanding (1946); and H. E. and
F. H. Wilson, *International Study of History Textbooks, 1955* (1956).

The Forms of Nationalistic Bias

I. THE NATURE OF MODERN NATIONALISTIC BIAS

Yet nationalistic bias is as persistent in today's schoolbooks as in those used a generation ago. More important, this bias is potentially more dangerous because it is less easy to detect. Usually it appears to stem not from any deliberate or conscious prejudice on the part of the author, but from the unconscious self. He writes against a background that allows him to see only one side of any story, no matter how hard he strives for objectivity. The age in which he lives, the training given him during his boyhood, the family that has reared him, the society in which he functions—all these and a hundred more forces operate constantly to inject in him views and values of which he is scarcely aware. Prejudices rooted in group misconceptions are less easy to guard against than those originating in individual bias. Yet these are the prejudices that appear on page after page of the textbooks used in today's secondary schools. That they should appear so regularly in the schoolbooks of two countries that speak the same language and have enjoyed a long period of friendship testifies to their durability.

In a shrinking world where nations must co-exist if they are to survive, the detection of nationalistic prejudice is of pressing importance to everyone. That this bias can ever be completely eliminated in a world of nation states is doubtful. Although there was much talk in the nineteenth century of 'objective' history, historians today agree that such a thing is impossible. No matter how dedicated the historian is to the unembroidered truth, that truth is forever beyond his grasp, for no two students can ever view the past through the same eyes, or speak of what they see with the same lips. Each individual subconsciously reveals his own beliefs and prejudices in every line that he writes. As long as men live within national boundaries, their environment will shape their prejudices. The historian views and records events relative to the time and place in which he lives. His goal of objectivity is constantly beyond his grasp, and his published works marred by prejudices that are a part of him as they are a part of the society that shaped his views.

This cannot be over-stressed if we are to be aware of nationalistic bias in the writings of historians or textbook authors.

Figures, it is said, do not lie, and historic dates are figures which seemingly tell the objective truth. But historians must put the dates together in meaningful form. Even though they may try hard not to weigh as well as count, their prejudices are bound to intrude, for dates significant in one country's history may be meaningless in another's. Scholars of two nationalities could no more agree on the most important dates in history than on the most important personalities or events. Ask two historians, one British and the other American, to list the half-dozen most important dates and events of the nineteenth century, and they might conceivably produce such a result as this:

British Historian	American Historian
1815 Defeat of Napoleon	1814 Treaty of Ghent
1832 First Reform Act	1831 Rise of Abolitionism
1846 Repeal of Corn Laws	1846 Mexican War
1854–8 Wars in Crimea and India	1861–5 Civil War
1867 Second Reform Act	1865–77 Reconstruction
1886 Home Rule Crisis	1887 Interstate Commerce Act
1899 Boer War	1898 Spanish-American War

Each historian would be perfectly honest in listing the events that seemed most important to him, yet they would disagree in every instance. Each would be mirroring the legitimate national concerns and the inevitable nationalistic prejudices of his own background. Dates, like figures, are meaningful only in context.

What we are saying is that facts never speak for themselves; they must be scrutinized critically no matter how coldly exact they appear. Whenever they have been arrayed on the pages of a history book they have been placed there by some person. He has selected which of the countless facts from mankind's record to include. In doing so he has deliberately or subconsciously chosen items that reflect his own individual interests, national prejudices, or the tensions of his own time and environment; he has arranged those facts in an order that may well convey a different meaning than would be reflected through another sequence and spacing. Textbooks are particularly suspect in this respect, for they are necessarily brief and the briefer the book the more rigorous the selection of facts to be included. 'The History we read,' says one eminent historian, 'though based on facts, is strictly speaking not factual at all, but a series of accepted judgments'. Judgments are personal, and no person is totally uncommitted.

Admittedly bias varies from nation to nation, from age to age, from circumstance to circumstance. It is often related to the amount of patriotic enthusiasm injected into the author by the system under which he lives. We are aware that the historical texts used in the schools of Nazi Germany were grossly distorted to glorify the Aryan myth, but we must remember that to the writers of those books there was no Aryan myth, only a scientifically proven truth of Nordic superiority. We know that pupils in the schools of Communist Russia or China today are taught that the 'people's democracy' will prevail over 'decadent capitalism', but our own schoolbooks glorify legislative democracy and our economic traditions with no less conviction and doubtless seem as distorted to communist readers as their books do to us.

Such blatant national bias is easy to detect (so long as it does not reflect our own involvements), but every author is guilty of the same manner of distortions in a lesser degree. All mirror the commonplace viewpoints concerning the past that are part of the mythology of every nation, and these commonplaces are dangerous things. Americans believe the United States won the War of 1812; Englishmen, assuming that they have heard of the war at all (and the need for this assumption is even more revealing), are sure that the Americans were soundly whipped; Canadians 'know' that they alone emerged with distinction. The histories of every nation reflect popular thought in exaggerating the importance of wars and battles that have been won, and minimizing or ignoring those that have been lost. Any reader of American textbooks will gain the impression that the American navy won a series of titanic battles against the British in the War of 1812 before mysteriously and unaccountably disappearing from the seas. This is natural, for these are the commonplace beliefs of the two nations. But, alas, the commonplaces of each country differ from the commonplaces of all other countries. Here is a source of bias that is not readily discernible but will plant distrust in those who read or listen.

4

2. THE FORMS OF NATIONALISTIC BIAS

All of this suggests that the detection of modern nationalistic bias is not easy. A textbook author seldom wears his prejudice proudly; more often he is unaware of any bias and will indignantly challenge the critics who charge that he is not completely objective. Yet nationalism has crept into the historical writing—and especially the textbooks—of every modern nation. In isolating such instances, we must equip ourselves with an understanding of the various forms in which bias exhibits itself. This can best be done by listing and defining the several types most frequently encountered:

(a) *Bias of Inertia*

This is properly not overt bias at all, but because it appears so frequently in textbook writing at all levels, and because the committee's investigations show it to be one of the most prominent sources of nationalistic distortion, it deserves to rank first in this catalogue. 'Bias by inertia' means the failure of textbook writers to keep abreast of current historical scholarship, and their consequent readiness to perpetuate on their pages outworn legends that usually exhibit nationalistic bias. It commonly takes the form of half-truths, which can be just as misleading as untruths.

The existence of this type of bias is easily understood. The borders of historical knowledge are being expanded so rapidly that no single person can hope to keep abreast of all new findings; simply to read the 500,000 pages published yearly on American history would require a rapid reader twenty-four hours a day for all 365 days of the year—and he would still be 60,000 pages behind when the year was over. Latest scholarly findings have to filter down to the textbook level slowly, usually appearing first in general monographs, then in the larger histories, and finally in textbooks. This process requires years so that texts are sometimes a generation behind in reflecting current historical views.

Compounding this crime is the tendency of all humans to think along well-worn lines rather than endure the intellectual torment needed to grasp new ideas. Historical distortions are passed on from generation to generation, from teacher to pupil, from textbook author to textbook author at all educational levels. This frailty perpetuates nationalistic bias, for the folklore of every nation glorifies its own heroes and degrades its enemies. American children are still taught that George Washington could not tell a lie, that Patrick Henry confounded George III with his shouted 'If this be treason, make the most of it', and that the United States never lost a war. English children learn that King John 'signed' the Magna Carta to start the world along the path to democracy, that Germany has always been opposed to freedom, and that the German chancellor in 1914 called the Belgium neutrality treaty a 'scrap of paper'. These are all half-truths at best; so long as textbook writers choose to employ them rather than seeking out the recent historical studies that have set the record straight, just so long will they contribute to nationalistic fervour.

Our investigations have shown that this cultural lag in text-book writing is a prominent source of distortion. In some books used in the United States today George III is still pictured as insane during the American Revolution, even though recent scholarship has shown him to be his normal self at that time. Modern authors are guilty only of ignorance in perpetuating this legend, for a generation ago historians on both sides of the Atlantic were sufficiently misled by their own Whig prejudices and the monarch's later mental illness to brand him a lunatic. Generations of British schoolboys have learned from their text-books that the American militiamen at Lexington Green fired the first shot of the Revolution, although students today agree that it is impossible to determine which side was guilty of this act. If school textbooks mirrored the meticulous research that is constantly changing our understanding of the past, they would be far less guilty of nationalistic bias.

In the United States, at least, authors have an opportunity to keep abreast of the scholarly world without the impossible task of reading the endless stream of journal articles and mono-graphs flowing from the presses. The Service Centre for Teachers of History, an agency of the American Historical Association, regularly publishes pamphlets summarizing the latest scholarly findings in various fields of historical study. In England the Historical Association provides a similar service on a more modest scale with its *Aids for Teachers* series of pamphlets. A wider use of these pamphlets, by textbook writers and publishers, as well as by teachers, is strongly recommended by the committee. Similarly the committee suggests that historical associations of other countries consider sponsoring similar series, as an effective device to combat this common form of nationalistic bias.

(b) *Unconscious Falsification*

This is a form of bias as frequently encountered as bias by inertia, and even more difficult to guard against. To write history free of national prejudice, textbook authors must divorce themselves from the milieu in which they have been reared and adopt points of view alien to their very nature. They must view their country's history through foreign eyes. They must burst the chrysalis of localism, and free themselves both from inherited cultural traditions and from much of what they have learned in their schooling. This is the most difficult of all assignments, and that few succeed is understandable. Yet until textbook writers can achieve this Olympian viewpoint, nationalism will creep unwittingly into their products.

Unconscious bias is rooted in the commonplaces of our lives. It is taught us at our mother's knee, deepened by the folktales of youth, strengthened by our early education, and perpetuated in our daily conversations with friends or strangers. Unknowingly we recite clichés which we accept unquestioningly, even though they are either rooted in falsehood or deliberate distortions. Englishmen will fight to the last Frenchmen, Americans are materialistic money-chasers, Orientals are inscrutable, Frenchmen keep mistresses. These are images that most of us accept, even though a moment of thought would reveal that the Battle of Britain was England's own, that American idealists are at least as numerous as dollar grabbers, that the Chinese are as open faced as their Occidental cousins, and that few Frenchmen could afford exotic feminine companionship even if they so desired. Yet untruths such as these influence and therefore mar historical writing.

The danger of subconscious falsification is compounded by the fact that the folklore of nationalism tends not only to degrade other nations but to glorify our own. The occasional French shopkeeper who refuses to speak English to his customers from overseas is not being consciously rude; he simply knows that the French language is more melodious, more expressive, and more understandable than any in the world. The American tourist who rudely asks 'what does this cost in money?' reflects a national belief that the dollar is both sound and recognizable, while all other currencies are both suspect and incomprehensible. Such attitudes mirror a dangerous complacency, aptly described by Nehru as 'the curious illusion of all peoples and all nations that in some way they are a chosen race'. This misconception is at times detectable as flagrant racialism: the Nordic Myth, the belief in Aryan superiority, the demands for a 'white man's world'. More dangerous, because less easily detected, is the unconscious assertion of national superiority that so often warps current historical writing. When the author of a fine book on national bias in historical textbooks can tell of 'a world in which *even* [italics ours] England counts for less than it did', we begin to realize that a national superiority complex is hard to guard against.

Historical writers can escape such bias only by immersing themselves so completely in the culture of the countries they are describing that they make the commonplaces of those lands their own. For the scholar who spends his whole life studying France from his London study or England from his American university office such a transmutation is sometimes possible. For the textbook writer it is not; he must necessarily base his knowledge on secondary works of such wide variety that he can never be sure of their freedom from error and animus. What English author of school-books can understand that the United States has not one but a complex of cultures shaped by differing environments and population patterns? What American teachers' college graduate, hoping to supplement his instructor's salary by a successful Junior High School history book, can appreciate the unique and influential role of the royal family in British culture and politics? Yet without such understandings, and thousands like them, textbook authors cannot escape misstatements and misunderstandings that reveal their own national prejudices. Unconscious falsification, whether resulting in the upgrading of the author's own nation or the downgrading of another of which he writes, is almost universal, and must be guarded against more than any other form of bias.

8

The Forms of Nationalistic Bias

(c) *Bias by Omission*

Historical writing above all is an exercise in selection. Spread before the historian is the multitudinous and diverse array of information that forms the record of man's past. From this he must select a relatively few items which can be arranged in the fashion needed to tell a meaningful story. Which items shall he select? How shall they be arranged? And how much weight should be given to each? The manner in which a textbook author answers these questions reveals not only his competence but also his national bias.

That nationalistic prejudice can be revealed by *which* facts an author selects is obvious. We have seen that the writers of English history textbooks when describing the War of 1812 describe one set of naval battles in which their vessels won while failing to mention equally numerous engagements in which they lost, and that American authors are so guilty of the same practice that a reader might think two separate wars were being discussed. These authors are not dishonest. Their books are free of overt errors of fact, but their story is far from the truth and they are as guilty of nationalistic distortion as the most out-and-out propagandist. The results of the sin of improper selection are as dangerous as those of the crime of deliberate falsification.

The national bias revealed by the *amount* of space used in describing any given episode is less obvious, but just as damaging. Authors who deliberately or subconsciously allot fuller treatment to events favourable to their own country than to those unfavourable reflect prejudice no less than those who omit one side of the story entirely. Textbook treatments of the American Revolution reveal this tendency. English books generally present a fuller picture of British victories than American, while relegating the battles at Saratoga and Yorktown to a few lines. Conversely American books devote a disproportionate amount of space to those triumphs, while ignoring the successful campaigns of General Charles Cornwallis in the South or General Washington's setbacks in the Middle Colonies. After all the war did not end after Saratoga or even after Yorktown.

The problem of space allotment is particularly clear in the comparative treatments of the War of 1812. Textbooks

9

published in the United States usually allot a full chapter to this contest; those printed in Britain dismiss it in a short paragraph or even a single line. Admittedly the war was from England's viewpoint an unimportant irritant, significant only because it forced a diversion of forces during the titanic Napoleonic struggles that were remaking the map of Europe. Viewed only in this light, the War of 1812 might properly be treated within those space limitations. But in another sense, that war was singularly important. Within the United States it unleashed the forces that led to a century of internal development; in Europe it launched an era of relative peace which allowed the American people to focus on their own problems of expansion and the exploitation of natural resources. No English schoolboy can understand the emergence of the United States as a major power without being familiar with this story. Nor can he appreciate the subsequent role of Canada within the British Empire unless he understands the change in Canadian-American relations that began as a result of the War of 1812. Yet that war is not adequately described in a single English textbook used today. Authors seeking to avoid nationalistic bias must be aware of proper space allotment no less than of deliberate misrepresentation.

(d) *Bias in Use of Language*

Because language excites responses it, like the selection of facts, may be used to create national misunderstanding. It may perpetuate derogatory epithets which engender a hostile impression of a nation or people in the reader's mind, or it may reveal subtle and often subconscious nuances that are scarcely noticeable but that through their cumulative effect create a sense of hostility. Let us examine these two types.

Openly derogatory language is easy to detect, but difficult to avoid for it often mirrors unconscious racial or nationalistic biases that are deeply rooted in various cultures. These clichés spring all too readily to the tongue, and appear all too often on the printed page. The 'Hessian mercenaries' who fought for Britain in the American Revolution were simply hired soldiers with less stomach for fighting than the British regulars, but that term transforms them into ogres bent on ravishing the countryside. We speak of 'Prussianism' and the 'Almighty Dollar' as though only the Germans were militaristic and only the Americans liked money. We refer to the peoples of the newly emerged African nations as 'colonials' or 'natives' or 'coloureds' or 'blacks' even though these terms betray a patronizing sense of superiority and are considered derogatory by the peoples to whom they are applied. As such they reveal a nationalistic as well as an ethnic bias that could easily be avoided.

Loaded language can be used to convert innocent sounding descriptions into instruments of propaganda. Witness this statement from a recent Russian publication dealing with the treatment of red Indians in the United States: 'The entire history of embattled America is one of unheard-of violence and treachery, or mass destruction of native peoples and their enslavement. The Indians resisted in despair but were defeated.' There is little actually inaccurate with that appraisal, and no modern American historian would defend the harsh policy that drove the red men from their homelands. But the use of such terms as 'mass destruction' and 'enslavement' creates the impression that a ruthless slaughter of Indians occupied the entire population of the United States for at least two centuries. There is nothing in the language used to suggest that this unhappy policy was formulated by a relatively few officials and enforced by a small number of frontiersmen.

These are examples of the deliberate or subconscious use of weighted words. More difficult to control or detect are the subtle nuances of language that so often distort the truth and fan the fires of nationalistic prejudice. Were the Americans who fought a revolution after 1776 'rebels' or 'patriots'? When an author speaks of 'slavery' does he suggest that a people were simply slaveholders, or does he imply the cruelty usually associated with that term? A writer who mentions 'democracy' means one thing in England, but does he mean the same thing when he writes against a Soviet background? There is a vast difference in meaning between 'execution' and 'murder'; between 'Indian' and 'savage'; between 'Southern Planter' and 'slave buyer'; between 'crowd' and 'mob'; between 'uprising' and 'riot'. A British textbook that ascribes the American Revolution to the 'actions of a determined minority' is conveying a far different (and more correct) impression of that struggle than the majority that employ the usual stereotypes: 'rebels' or 'patriots'.

Only by constant vigilance in choosing just the right word for the right place, and by constant awareness to detect the subtle changes in word meaning as they cross national boundaries, can this semantic foundation for nationalistic bias be eliminated. Teachers and writers alike should remember that words change their meaning a great deal over a period of years as they do in translation or in moving from country to country speaking the same language. Translation from one language to another may be no more fruitful of deception, however unwitting, than from eighteenth-century English into twentieth-century American, and from an atmosphere of peace to an atmosphere of tension.

(e) *Bias by Cumulative Implication*

This formidable title can be explained thus: a textbook writer without violating the canons of truth can assign such an array of virtues to his own country that the reader is left unaware that other nations made some contribution to the world's civilization. Such an author is guilty of presenting only one side of a many sided story; he may also be charged with contributing to the sense of national superiority that is objectivity's most dangerous enemy.

Examples of this type of bias are numerous, but some of the best are found in the history of inventions. To many an English textbook writer, the basic credit for splitting the atom goes solely to Lord Rutherford of Cambridge; Danish texts award the honour to Niels Bohr, German to Otto Hahn or Lise Meitner, Italian to Enrico Fermi, and American to Ernest Lawrence and the team of physicists which first released the power of the atom at the University of Chicago during World War II. No one of these statements is wrong for each of these men made his contribution. Yet to single out any one as *the* hero is to obscure the fact that nuclear energy was harnessed by an international, not a national, effort.

Every field of history can be—and has been—abused by textbook authors who parade evidence favourable to their own country while obscuring the contribution of others. Some American textbooks describe the French and Indian War with barely a mention of the role of Britain and Prussia on the Continent, the American Revolution without recognizing that victory would have been almost certainly impossible without French aid, the War of 1812 with insufficient credit to France for preventing a concentration of British power against the United States, the world wars of the twentieth century without properly emphasizing the major burden borne by the Allies before and during American participation. The result is a distortion of history; the student reader emerges with the impression that his own nation has monopolized progress, single-handedly turned back the enemies of civilization, and is alone equipped to lead the world along the path to a righteous future. By tracing one strand alone of the complex warp and woof of man's record, an author has denied his readers adequate knowledge of the part played by other peoples. He has failed to reveal that internationalism, rather than nationalism, has been responsible for much past progress.

These, then, are the forms in which national bias most frequently appears in today's textbooks. Authors can be indicted for an intellectual sluggishness that leads them to repeat the outworn clichés of the past rather than relay the findings of modern scholarship; for an unconscious falsification that throws into relief the commonplace misunderstandings and distortions that are part of all national heritages; for the conscious or subconscious selection and arrangement of information to glorify their own land at the expense of others; for the employment of weighted language that upgrades their own country and degrades others; and for a tendency to magnify the contributions of their own nation by parading its accomplishments while neglecting the no less important achievements of other countries.

This formidable array of charges should not be taken to mean that today's textbooks are deliberate propaganda documents, or even that they seriously distort the story of Anglo-American relations. Most authors are well intentioned, but some are apparently guilty of a desire—conscious or subconscious—to glorify their own nation. The purpose of this report is not to castigate these writers for their sins. They are human, and humans are prey to subconscious prejudices and victims of commonplace beliefs that are almost impossible to uproot. Some, moreover, who write for an American audience, are subjected to social pressures not inflicted on their English counterparts. Instruction in American history is defined in the United States as a national duty, designed to plant the seeds of patriotism in youth. When the *purpose* of a textbook is nationalistic, its tone will mirror that purpose. Yet loyalty to one's country can be taught without breeding dislike of other nations, and of this textbook authors in the United States have been guilty. The chapters that follow will attempt to prove this point, and perhaps to aid writers in achieving that freedom from bias that must be the goal of all historians.

II
ENGLISH AND AMERICAN
SECONDARY EDUCATION

SIMPLY to thumb the pages of any history textbook used in the secondary schools of England or the United States makes clear the wide difference in aims, methods, and philosophy of the two educational systems. American textbooks are unabashedly designed to attract readers; they are encased in multicoloured covers, printed in large type on glossy paper, and so larded with maps, charts, and illustrations in rainbow hues that the most lethargic dullard could scarcely resist their appeal. Textbooks used in the secondary schools of England and Wales are, in contrast, usually pridefully drab; they are enclosed within workmanlike covers, printed in type that tempts the middle-aged to reach for magnifying glasses, and often scornfully free of virtually all illustrations save a few line drawings. Even the titles mirror their differences. American books proclaim themselves as *This Is America's Story*, *America Land of Freedom*, or *Our Free Nation*. England's are content with *British and Foreign History: Book Three*, or *From George III to George VI: A Brief History of Britain from 1760 to 1952*.

These variations underline the fact that neither English nor American textbooks can be judged outside of the milieu for which they have been intended. A volume deliberately designed to attract readers must deal differently with historical episodes than one written with the knowledge that it would be crammed down pupils' intellectual gullets. A study of the American Revolution or the First World War planned for the use of sophisticated young people eighteen or nineteen years old could scarcely be expected to resemble one aimed at a group somewhat younger in years and culturally less mature. To compare books with these differing aims and audiences is certainly unfair and probably impossible.

To understand the variant problems of textbook writers in England and the United States, a reader must also understand the philosophy and methods of secondary education in the two countries. The following chapter, although admittedly superficial, may be helpful to those seeking such an understanding. It deals first with the nature of secondary schools in England and Wales on the one hand and the United States on the other, secondly with the nature of history instruction in the two nations, and finally with the purposes of historical studies in the secondary schools.

I. THE SECONDARY SCHOOLS OF ENGLAND AND WALES

British law requires compulsory school attendance for all between the ages of five and fifteen; plans call for extending the upper limit to sixteen years by 1970. Parents may choose to send their children either to a *State* school where education is free or to a school where they have to pay fees.

(a) *State Schools*

Several types of state schools exist: grammar schools, technical secondary schools, secondary modern schools, and bilateral and comprehensive schools. Our interest is in two of these—grammar schools and secondary modern schools—where most instruction in history takes place.

Grammar schools provided virtually all secondary education until nearly the end of the nineteenth century; today they offer a traditional type of schooling and prepare an increasing number of boys and girls for the universities. A majority of their students remain in school after the compulsory age of fifteen and a steadily increasing proportion stay until they are eighteen or over. *Secondary Modern schools* care for the great majority of English children, most of whom leave school as early as legally possible although the numbers staying on for an additional year is gaining fast.

Students are selected for one or the other of these schools by various means but hitherto largely on the basis of a competitive examination in English, arithmetic, and intelligence which is

named the 'Eleven Plus' from the age at which it is taken.
Those who do well on this gruelling test are sent to Grammar
schools, those who do less well are destined for the Secondary
Modern schools. Decisions at this point are made by the Local
Education Authorities (the LEA's as they are generally known),
i.e. the education committees of county or county borough
councils which are responsible for operating the state schools
provided by the community. Each LEA decides what proportion of its children it is willing to admit to Grammar
schools, with the figures varying broadly from 10 per cent to
40 per cent. An increasing number of LEA's are ruling that no
children be sent to Grammar schools, but that all must attend a
Comprehensive school combining the functions and purposes
of the Grammar and Secondary Modern schools, in effect
abandoning the 'Eleven Plus' examination.

In the state schools of England and Wales at the beginning
of 1963 rather under a million and a half children of the compulsory secondary school age-range (eleven to fifteen years)
attended Secondary Modern schools (65·5%), less than half a
million attended Grammar schools (19·2%), and some 340,000
were distributed among other types of schools (15·3%).

(b) *Fee-paying Schools*

Of the 2,700,000 children in England and Wales between
the ages of eleven and fifteen in 1963, some 8·3 per cent
attended schools where fees were paid. Most of these schools
would be called 'private' schools in the United States. Two
types—the *Direct Grant* schools and the *Independent* schools—play
an important role in the English educational system.

The *Direct Grant* schools, a curious kind of hybrid, allot from
one-quarter to one-half of their places to children in the area
whose fees are paid by the LEA's; the remainder of their pupils
pay charges scaled to the income of their parents. The difference
between these sums and the cost of education is made up by
direct grants from the central government. These schools, some
of which are called Grammar schools, are notable for the
quality of their academic instruction and for the high proportion of their pupils who qualify for entrance to a university.

The *Independent* schools are largely sustained by fees paid by
parents of the pupils. The best known of these are the boys'

17

Public Schools such as Eton, Winchester and Rugby which typify English education to foreigners. They are actually fewer in numbers than their influence suggests; some two hundred are represented in the Headmasters' Conference which most strictly defines a 'Public School', whereas there are altogether about 1,500 Independent schools in England and Wales teaching boys and girls of the eleven to fifteen age-range. Normally admission to a Public School follows intensive training at a preparatory boarding school, and is at the age of thirteen or more, rather than at eleven as in the state secondary schools. The educational program is basically designed to train for entrance to Oxford or Cambridge universities, although only a minority of their pupils proceed thither.

2. THE SECONDARY SCHOOLS OF THE UNITED STATES

Unlike England, the United States has no national school requirements; instead compulsory attendance is controlled by the states. Normally state law requires school attendance for all children between the ages of six and sixteen, although six states specify attendance through the age of seventeen and four through eighteen. Students at the secondary level may choose between two types of schools, the *Public* or state supported schools, and the *Nonpublic* schools were fees are required save for those awarded private scholarships.

(a) *Public Schools*

Both Public and Nonpublic schools in the United States are graded, with grades I to XII. Normally a child enters grade I at the age of six, sometimes after preliminary training in a kindergarten. During the first six grades he is in a Primary or Grammar school; in grades VII and VIII he is in a Junior High school, and in grades IX through XII in a High school. Normally a pupil enters the Junior High school at the age of eleven or twelve, and the High school at the age of thirteen or fourteen, completing his secondary education with graduation from grade XII at the age of eighteen. Students in these two schools correspond most closely with those in the Grammar, Secondary Modern, and Public Schools of England and Wales.

English and American Secondary Education

The structure of the American educational system can be understood only in its historical context. It originated during the first half of the nineteenth century on the state level, for constitutional restrictions as then interpreted denied the national government authority to support education directly. This tradition has been maintained, with state and local—not federal—agencies providing tax funds for the support of schools. Local control has resulted in a wide variation in educational standards. These are established by a number of local and state authorities: state legislatures, state departments of education, local school boards, and local administrations. School boards which are charged with allotting tax funds and establishing educational policies within local areas, are normally elected by the people. They are provided with funds largely through local property taxes, but with some aid from the state treasury.

When the American educational system originated in the nineteenth century, primary schooling was considered sufficient for all save the few who aspired to professional training. As the social order became more complex with industrialization late in the century, demands increased for more training at state expense. The High school resulted from this pressure, first gaining prominence in the 1890's. Thus it is a recent graft on the American educational system, in contrast to the English Grammar school which is as old as the monarchy and common law, and far older than Parliament.

This historical evolution explains why the United States has no complex of state-supported schools such as England and Wales, and why no 'Eleven Plus' examinations are needed to determine a pupil's future. Instead students normally progress from grades I through XII, save for those who are forced to repeat a grade before going on, or those who drop out at the end of compulsory school age.

In recent years social complexities have sparked a demand to separate the better from the more ordinary pupils, much as the 'Eleven Plus' examination has hitherto done in England. Instead of setting up special schools for superior students, however, the larger High schools in the United States have provided more advanced instruction for this group by placing them in separate classes, known as 'honors courses' or 'advanced placement

19

courses'. The latter allow students to receive credit for university courses before they go on to a university.

(b) *Nonpublic schools*

In 1962 some 9,500,000 pupils were enrolled in the public High schools of the United States. An additional 1,200,000 were in nonpublic schools, in which fees were required save for those earning scholarships.

Many types of nonpublic schools exist in the United States, but two are particularly important: the *Parochial High schools* and the *Academies*. *Parochial High schools* are maintained by numerous religious bodies, but particularly by Roman Catholic and Lutheran churches. Normal secular education comparable to that obtained in a public High school is provided, plus religious instruction. *Academies* are privately endowed and supported institutions, comparable to the English Public Schools, and designed usually to train pupils for admission to college or university. Admission to some of the better-known academies—such as Phillips Andover, Phillips Exeter, Groton School, or Lawrenceville School—is on a highly competitive basis, allowing educational programs to be of an advanced level.

Both the Parochial High schools and the Academies are graded like public schools, and maintain similar educational programs, employing for the most part the same sort of textbooks. In a few of the better Academies, as in some of the better High schools in populous urban or suburban areas, textbooks normally designed for use in universities are used, just as they are in the top forms of English grammar schools or Public Schools. These, however, are the exception.

3. THE TEACHER IN BRITISH AND AMERICAN SECONDARY EDUCATION

The quality of teachers recruited into classrooms, and the nature and extent of their education, obviously influence their use or abuse of textbooks. So does the degree of freedom that the teacher is allowed in selecting his own teaching techniques and materials. These vary greatly between the two nations.

In England and Wales nearly 75 per cent of the teachers in Grammar schools in 1962 were university graduates; in the

Secondary Modern schools the proportion was only 17 per cent. In the United States teacher requirements vary greatly from community to community. In general, High school teachers in urban areas possess a college or university degree; in the larger city High schools many will have earned a Master of Arts degree in addition. Elsewhere, and especially in predominantly rural states, a year or more of college preparation beyond High school will qualify an individual for a teacher's certificate.

The nature of teacher training, as well as the quantity, also varies greatly between England and Wales and the United States. English university education is dedicated to providing factual knowledge and interpretative skills in the particular subject-matter of the student's specialization. A young man or woman leaving a university to begin Grammar school teaching after three years of 'reading' history should possess a competent knowledge of his or her subject, whether or not additional professional training followed. In the United States, on the other hand, teachers can qualify for Junior High school and High school posts with a degree from a teachers' college where the emphasis is on methods rather than subject matter. Such an individual, while competent to handle and even inspire a class, would not be equipped to select a proper textbook in history, or to challenge that textbook when it was wrong.

Perhaps reflecting these differences in training, the authority granted the secondary school teacher to select and employ educational materials varies greatly between the two nations. In England and Wales, teachers in individual schools decide what they are going to teach and how they will teach it, with no interference from national or local authorities. Only occasionally does a Local Education Authority restrict this freedom by preparing an approved list from which textbooks must be selected; in practice this means nothing for the list customarily includes every text that might be employed. The responsibility of the teacher to choose his own textbooks is taken for granted and cheerfully accepted; it is but seldom abused, for tradition, common sense, and inertia govern the choice of the books no less than individual initiative.

One restraint on freedom of textbook selection in England and Wales stems from the emphasis on nationally administered —or 'external'—written examinations which are believed to provide objective evidence of the pupils' achievement in the later stages of secondary education. Much the most important of these is the General Certificate of Education (GCE) set by eight different examining boards connected in varying ways with the universities. This is a 'subject' examination in several fields, taken at Ordinary Level (O Level) by pupils aged about sixteen, and at Advanced Level (A Level) by those about eighteen. The influence of these examinations in setting and maintaining academic standards has been immense, and inevitably they have done much to shape and determine (some would say petrify) the subject materials and textbooks used in secondary schools. Until recently their influence was largely confined to Grammar schools, but the GCE examinations are increasingly employed in Secondary Modern schools; one of every nine pupils taking the examinations in 1962 came from these schools. Despite their standardizing effects, the teacher in the secondary schools of England and Wales has far greater freedom to search out the materials and techniques needed to inspire his students than in the United States.

American practices in textbook selection vary greatly from state to state and community to community, but rarely save in a few outstanding High schools or Academies does the teacher have freedom to do exactly what he wishes. Normally the state or local Board of Education selects a list of 'approved' textbooks in each subject; one or more of these books will then be chosen in each High school, either by the principal of the school, or by a committee of teachers, or both. The 'approved list' in each state or community is selected by a tortuous process involving the assent of a whole hierarchy of committees and individuals.

Thus in one typical state the Board of Education each May 1 names fifteen persons from a list submitted by the state Commissioner of Education to serve as a State Textbook Committee. Normally those asked to serve are experienced and active educators. This committee studies the books submitted by publishers, and recommends to the Commissioner of Education a complete list of textbooks approved for adoption at the various grade levels. The Commissioner, if he desires, may remove books from this list. He then submits it to the state Board of Education which also makes such deletions as it wishes. This done, the Board places contracts with the successful publishers to provide textbooks to the state for from one to six years. Within each school district a committee of teachers selects from the multiple lists the specific books that will be used as textbooks in its schools. After a school is supplied with the chosen texts, they must be used for the duration of the contract period.

Procedures such as this, followed throughout the United States on the state or local level, deny the individual instructor the right to select the textbook that seems most suitable to his needs. They also influence the manner of textbook writing in America, and have a bearing on the nationalistic tone of the books.

4. THE TEACHING OF HISTORY IN BRITISH SECONDARY SCHOOLS

The relative freedom from regulation in English secondary schools precludes generalizations on either the quantity or quality of instruction in history. There are no official requirements, national or local, such as those found in every American state. An English secondary school could, in theory, teach no history at all, although custom requires that all emphasize the subject. Normally, however, in Grammar schools all pupils study history throughout the first three years of the five-year course leading to the O Level General Certificate of Education examination; for the remaining two years history is often an 'optional' subject that is still widely elected. During these three years when history is required, from two to three weekly periods of approximately forty-five minutes are devoted to the subject; after the O Level examination when history becomes a specialist subject for the minority who elect it the instructional time is increased to six or eight periods weekly. In the Secondary Modern schools most pupils study history throughout their course, and the time allotted to it per week is slightly greater.

The nature of the history studied in the secondary schools of England and Wales varies greatly; today, moreover, many teachers are paying greater attention to non-British and recent history than has been customary in the past. But British history is usually the staple of the studies leading to the O Level examination, and very frequently the nineteenth and twentieth centuries are the periods selected for special emphasis. Insomuch as a chronological approach is usually favoured, the result is a course of study something like this for the period to the O Level examinations:

1st year Either Ancient World or Middle Ages
2nd year Middle Ages or Tudors and Stuarts
3rd year Tudors and Stuarts or Eighteenth Century
4th year Eighteenth Century or Nineteenth Century
5th year (O Level) Nineteenth and Early Twentieth Centuries

This leads to odd results, especially for pupils who do not offer history for the O Level examinations, and so do not study the subject after the third year; many able young Englishmen and women go through life without detailed knowledge of their nation's history after the Glorious Revolution or the death of Queen Anne.

5. THE TEACHING OF HISTORY IN AMERICAN SECONDARY SCHOOLS

Courses in United States history are required by law in virtually all the fifty states. Students must pass such courses to be promoted from Junior High school to High school, and again to graduate from High school; in many states they must also successfully complete examinations on the national and state constitutions. These requirements force teachers to dedicate a sizeable portion of the curriculum to the subject.

During his twelve years in primary and secondary schools, the average pupil takes a course in American history three times. In Grade V the subject is presented in broad terms, with stress on exploration and discovery, biographies of important Americans, and the westward movement with its symbols: log cabins, covered wagons, Indians, cowboys, and goldseekers. The subject is normally allotted fifty minutes each day, while English studies occupy a somewhat longer time period and a variety of other subjects—mathematics, science and health, art, music, and physical education—are assigned somewhat smaller portions of the school day.

In Grade VIII, taken in Junior High school, United States history is repeated, with greater emphasis on a textbook, and with the whole span from Columbus to modern times under scrutiny. Normally the stress at this level is on social rather than political or economic history, and with field trips, class projects, and written or oral reports supplementing regular instruction. Usually six or eight weeks are set aside for the study of national and state constitutions, to equip the student for the examinations that he must pass before entering High school. The history course is allotted about fifty minutes of each school day, with a comparable time spent on English, science, mathematics, and a foreign language. Physical education, and a minor subject such as music, typing, photography, workshop, or home economics also claim a share of each pupil's time. Ordinarily the 'home room' teacher gives instruction in history and English, while the other subjects are taught by specialists in those fields, in contrast with the primary grades where one teacher teaches all subjects.

The final course in American history, taken in grade XI or XII of High school, again retraces the history of the United States from Columbus to the present, with the use of a textbook, supplementary reading in documents and secondary works, and a wider use of library facilities. Stress is placed on economic, diplomatic, and social aspects, but political and military history are not neglected. Once more three to six weeks are usually set aside for the study of state and national constitutions, to equip the student for the further examinations that he must pass to graduate from High school. A typical student at this level would take, in addition to his history course, three or four other 'major' subjects, such as English, mathematics, a foreign language, and a laboratory science, plus 'electives' and physical education. All classes meet daily for forty or fifty minutes.

In addition to his triple indoctrination in United States history, the usual schoolboy in America is subjected to a wider diet of general historical studies than his cousin in the secondary schools of England and Wales. History instruction offered a typical pupil would follow such a pattern as this:

7th grade World History
8th grade United States History
9th grade World History to 1700 or Civics
10th grade World History since 1700 or Ancient and Medieval
11th grade Modern European or American History
12th grade United States History or American History Problems

In addition, larger schools might offer students in their last two

25

years a choice of courses in Russian history, British history, Latin American history, or Far Eastern history. These, together with all history courses except those in United States history, would be 'electives', and not required of students.

This brief survey suggests that in both English and American secondary schools, history instruction plays a prominent part in the 'syllabus' (as the British would put it) or 'curriculum' (as the Americans would say). It also suggests that history teachers in Grammar and Secondary Modern schools in England and Wales are better equipped to select, use, and dispute textbooks than their counterparts in the United States. Nearly all in the Grammar schools, and some in the Secondary Modern schools, are university graduates with degrees in history, while the non-university graduates who teach history in Secondary Modern schools have probably done a specialist course in the subject (in addition to a course in method) at a Teachers' Training College. In the United States, in contrast, the history teacher at the Junior High school level teaches at least two subjects, and only rarely can be judged to have an expert knowledge of history. Even in High school, where the history teacher usually confines himself to that subject (except in a few schools whose administrators believe that anyone knows American history and delegates its teaching to the basketball coach or the Latin instructor whose enrollment is insufficient to keep him busy), training has been more often in methodology than subject matter. Teachers with such scant knowledge of their discipline will be more inclined to lean heavily on a textbook, and to sanctify it as the gospel, than will teachers in England and Wales who may use a text only as a foil for the expression of their own views.

6. THE PURPOSES OF ENGLISH AND AMERICAN HISTORY TEACHING

The purposes of history teaching in English schools are not easy to define. A recent pamphlet, *Teaching History* (1952 and often reprinted), published by the Ministry of Education, in discussing this matter suggested that there had been two traditional purposes: the inculcation of a moral example, and the bestowing of a national heritage. Yet its authors went on to say that these were now being overtaken by a third purpose of a very different kind: the deliberate use of history as a means of enlarging the pupil's imaginative experience.

Certainly teachers of history in English schools differ widely in their interpretation of the purpose and value of their subject in the classroom. Some would reject the idea of using history as a source of individual moral example; others would condemn the suggestion that school history should be the vehicle of patriotism. Nevertheless, in general it seems fair to say that beneath the rich variety of individual differences there is a great area of common ground.

The vast majority of those who teach the subject in English schools find its value in the contribution it can make to the development of the individual human being. They see it as a means of awakening and stimulating his imagination and of enlarging his sympathies; as providing a training in a particular kind of accuracy and as encouraging the growth of a balanced outlook; as giving some basic understanding of the operation of cause and effect in human society; and ultimately as a source, if not of wisdom itself, at any rate of cultivating the kind of understanding which may lead to wisdom. Obviously this approach does not exclude the belief that history may provide a training in citizenship; most English teachers of history—although certainly not all—would probably claim that much of what they teach, both in knowledge and more importantly in attitude of mind, is a necessary element in training their pupils for a full place in contemporary society. Yet they see such training only as a part of the cultivation of the whole man.

In marked contrast with this attitude, both educators in the United States and a majority of the people view instruction in the nation's history as a practical, pragmatic means of protecting and preserving the American way of life. This attitude is explainable only within the context of the history of education in the United States. During the early part of the nineteenth century, when the nation was forced to decide between a system of public or privately supported schools, the principal argument of those who favoured state support was the necessity of schooling to produce a literate electorate. The fate of democracy, they insisted, was related to the degree of education among the voters. Insomuch as the government would be the principal beneficiary of a school system, support for that system should come from government. In the beginning, then, schools were viewed as practical devices rather than cultural assets.

This view has persisted down to the present. Today, as in the 1830's, the purpose of American education is to instill loyalty to country into the nation's youth and to educate future citizens into the wise use of the franchise. Education was, and is, looked upon as citizenship training and as a means of safeguarding and extending democracy. This functional view obviously influences the nature of American history textbooks and the form of classroom instruction. On the one hand a tendency exists to make the textbook more nationalistic than in some other nations, for its avowed purpose is to strengthen patriotism. On the other, local pressure groups, often more nationalistic than the authors or users of textbooks, are in a position to bring pressure on school boards and adopting commissions to select texts mirroring their own point of view. The local direction of American schools has made them vulnerable to dominant local interests which do not necessarily reflect the attitudes of the community as a whole. In practice, this results in a deviation toward a more nationalistic approach to history.

This brief survey of the nature and purpose of history teaching in the United States and England and Wales makes one fact indisputably clear: the textbooks of the two nations cannot be exactly compared. The English books used in O Level classes have no particular patriotic or functional purpose; they are designed for teachers versed in the subject matter and capable of using the text as a springboard to the teaching of information and interpretations somewhat more sophisticated than the book itself. American books are written for a mass audience where 'adoption' by a single state can bring a fortune to author and publisher; they are written to indoctrinate the young with the virtues of Americanism and to create an informed electorate; they are to be used by teachers who often have little professional training in history and must rely on the textbook to inform them as well as their students.

Against this backdrop of differences, we can now turn to the textbooks themselves, to note how they reflect the purposes and philosophies of the two nations in their attitudes towards nationalism.

III

THE AMERICAN REVOLUTION

THIS chapter and the next two will describe the national bias detected in the textbook treatment of the three episodes selected for analysis: the American Revolution, the War of 1812, and the First World War. They will necessarily vary in length; the Revolution still inspires more patriotic enthusiasm than later episodes in Anglo-American history, with a corresponding multiplication of the errors of bias. This subject, too, receives a more generous space allotment by writers on both sides of the Atlantic; bias in the textbook treatment of the War of 1812 manifests itself largely by the failure of British writers to discuss the subject, and of the First World War by the refusal of both British and American authors to recognize the contributions made by the other nation to the outcome. Grievous as these faults are, they do not lend themselves to extensive or detailed description.

In discussing each of these episodes, its treatment in the American Junior High school textbooks will be described first, then its fate at the hands of authors of texts used in the Senior High schools of the United States, and finally the manner in which it is treated in texts used in the Grammar and Secondary Modern schools of England and Wales. This admittedly is not an ideal organization; fairness requires that comparison be made between books designed for the same age level. Such a division is difficult with English books. Educators who appraise them use such phrases as: 'aimed at the lower forms of Grammar Schools, and would probably be regarded as too difficult for Secondary Modern Schools', 'much used in the middle forms of Grammar Schools,' 'a Secondary Modern book,' 'used in Preparatory Schools, Secondary Modern Schools, and in the junior classes of Grammar Schools,' 'intended for older pupils

29

taking the O-Level GCE Examination, but designed for the weaker candidates among these,' or 'a better Secondary Modern book but the language is a bit difficult.' Clearly English textbooks are aimed at all levels of comprehension, with the gradations between them so minute as to make clear division impossible. Hence all such books have been lumped together, even though American textbooks have been divided into those used in Junior High schools and High schools.

I. AMERICAN JUNIOR HIGH SCHOOL TEXTBOOKS[1]

These provide an admirable introduction to the study of national bias in history texts, for they exhibit patriotic prejudices to a degree not found in American High school or English Secondary school textbooks. Several commonly used in Junior High schools of the United States are so blatantly nationalistic that they seem designed to propagandize rather than instruct.

(a) *Causes of the American Revolution*

Fortunately, the tone of most books is not that of one that entitles its chapter on the origins of the war 'The Colonies Unite to Resist British Oppression', but even those that exercise greater moderation are guilty of sins of omission and commission that seriously distort the truth. Omissions can be as damaging to international understanding as the most unwarranted self-glorification. Texts that try to make the outbreak of the Revolution understandable to pupils without mentioning such things as the advantages to the colonies of the British trade system, Pontiac's Rebellion, the Proclamation of 1763, the Sugar and Currency Acts, constitutional and commercial issues, and the internal conflicts within the colonies present Hamlet without the Prince of Denmark. Yet one or more (and sometimes several) of these items were omitted from every textbook examined. Very few books, furthermore, attempted to set the preliminaries of the Revolution against the background in America, Britain, and the European world, and still fewer attempted to go behind commonly recited incidents—the Stamp

---

[1] For a list of Junior High school textbooks analysed and cited in this section, see Preface, p. xi.

Act, the Boston Massacre, the Tea Party, and such—to the fundamental changes occurring alike in the colonies and Britain.

Nor are errors of commission lacking. Underlying most of these is a subconscious assumption of American superiority; leaders of the Revolutionary cause are endowed with virtues that their enemies completely lack, and Revolutionary soldiers with abilities that are obviously not shared by the British. American militiamen did contribute to England's victory over France in the French and Indian War (although not nearly so much as they should). But to state that 'they had proved to British soldiers and officers that a colonist could fight as well and as bravely as any man' is to employ nuances of language that glorify one group at the expense of another. To say that 'they also showed the British how to fight in the frontier fashion' is a positive mis-statement; historians now know that European-trained infantry could not be converted into frontier fighters overnight.

Modern scholars have long known that the Proclamation of 1763 was a measure needed to still an Indian uprising as well as solve other pressing western problems, that it was hurriedly prepared to meet an emergency situation, and that it was designed to restrain westward migration only temporarily until the interior tribes could be pacified and pushed aside. Yet these essential facts are apparently unknown to most of the textbook writers; they see the Proclamation as an unjust royal decree aimed at banning frontiersmen forever from the trans-Appalachian West and a just cause for rebellion. One only compounds error by adding that under the measure 'the British government would get all the wealth created by the development of the frontier'.

Even more serious is the failure of textbook writers to paint an accurate picture of the commercial conflict between Britain and her colonies. These regulations were nearly four centuries old when the colonists first began their protests; even those that upset the Americans most had graced the statute books for nearly one hundred years. Yet pupils are led to believe that they had been but recently adopted, as part of the repressive pattern emerging under George III. Nor do textbook authors show, as historians have long recognized, that these Navigation

Acts were designed partly to benefit colonial trade and ship-building. Too often the reader is told that the acts were aimed against the colonies, not against foreign countries as was really the case. Too often he is led to believe that the measures robbed Americans of the freedom to buy and sell in world markets, without any explanation that their trade had been almost as restricted by economic barriers before the laws were passed, and that losses were compensated by commercial privileges within the British empire. Much colonial prosperity in the first half of the eighteenth century was traceable to the mono-poly enjoyed within England and the booming shipbuilding industry encouraged by the Navigation Acts.

If these trade measures fare badly at the hands of Junior High school textbook writers, so does the British monarch, George III. 'He had,' one author notes, 'been trained by his mother who often said to him, "George, be King!" When he came to the throne he tried to put her teachings into effect. . . . He did not believe that the wishes or rights of the colonists should interfere with the growing power of the British govern-ment, of which he was the head.' Yet historians have known for a generation that George's mother never gave him such advice, and that the king was a sincere advocate of progress, struggling for an honest and efficient government rather than for tyrannical power. That he possessed only modest abilities, and that he was caught in the mesh of a political situation that rendered his efforts ineffective, is no justification for branding him an iron-willed ruler determined to coerce his colonial subjects.

Parliament fares as badly as George III at the hands of textbook authors. One marvellously distorts the truth when he compresses the complex story of that body's financial measures into three simple sentences:

> Colonial trade would be controlled more strictly than ever before. British soldiers would be stationed in great numbers and live among the colonists. New taxes would draw money from the colonies to the mother country.

What hostile impressions are conjured up by such weighted language: 'great numbers' of troops sent to 'live among' the people, who are to pay for their own oppression. No reader

ENGLISH COLONIAL POLICY

STEPS TAKEN BY THE ENGLISH TO GOVERN THE COLONIES AND TO MAKE MONEY FROM TRADE	STEPS TAKEN BY THE COLONISTS TO PROTECT THEIR OWN INTERESTS AND TO SAFEGUARD LIBERTY
TRADE AND NAVIGATION ACTS *LED TO*	SMUGGLING GOODS
THE STAMP ACT *LED TO*	FIRES AND RIOTS
THE TOWNSHEND ACT *LED TO*	THE VIRGINIA RESOLUTIONS
THE TAX ON TEA *LED TO*	THE BOSTON TEA PARTY

1. Modern drawing used in a Junior High School textbook in the United States, suggesting a series of British acts of aggression which incited the colonists to revolution.

2. Cartoon from a popular Junior High School textbook used in the United States, showing foppish-looking Britains planning to enrich their land at the expense of the colonists, and indignant Americans righteously protesting.

could even guess the truth: that the soldiers were to guard the frontiers, that a major portion of their cost was to be borne by British taxpayers, that the quartering of troops was an accepted practice in Britain and America, and that the colonists had been given opportunity to propose alternatives before the revenue measures were enacted. Verbal distortions such as these perpetuate the 'devil' theory of history by giving pliable young readers an image of British villainy and American innocence.

The Stamp Act is discussed in most textbooks with some attempt at impartiality; people in the United States today are so accustomed to stamp duties of assorted kinds that they can hardly be painted as iniquitous. Yet many are guilty of damning omissions that threaten the case for objectivity. Few texts point out that stamp duties were a traditional and often-used taxation device in Britain. One distorts the truth in saying that 'Franklin and other agents from other colonies tried to persuade Grenville not to have the Stamp Act passed;' actually the colonial agents were as surprised by American opposition as George III's ministers. Another adds ignorance to injury by suggesting that revenue from the measure was to be used to pay royal governors, when nothing could be further from the truth. Nor does any author even mention the concept of 'virtual representation' which in some Englishmen's eyes endowed the Stamp Act and other revenue measures with legal sanctity.

Colonial opposition to the Stamp Act receives thorough— perhaps too thorough—attention in all Junior High school textbooks. A perennial favourite is Patrick Henry's speech to the Virginia House of Burgesses in which he allegedly cried: 'Caesar had his Brutus, Charles I his Cromwell, and George III may profit by their example. If this be treason make the most of it.' Scarcely an author can resist repeating that bit of folklore, even though historians have long known that Henry's heroic words originated in the imagination of nineteenth-century writers rather than in his own patriotism. Despite the ample space given to this outworn legend, writers seem to lack room to picture American resistance as the lawless defiance of authority that it was; they rarely describe the rioting, the mob destruction, and the abuses to which the Stamp agents were subjected. One author tells how the resistance groups 'circulated printed statements against the Stamp Act, held picnics and patriotic rallies, and denounced British politics'—suggesting a wrist-slapping sort of protest that hardly mirrors the property destruction and tarring-and-feathering that really took place. Textbooks also fail to give proper weight to the Declaratory Act (a definition of Parliamentary supremacy), and assign too much to the role of British merchants in securing the measure's repeal, judgments that disagree with modern historical interpretations.

The second major set of revenue laws, the Townshend Acts, are treated no more objectively. Charles Townshend himself, although never 'head of the British government' as one writer believes, is the villain of the piece, pictured as 'unfriendly to the colonists', and the author of legislation that 'went further than the Stamp Act had ever gone'. Modern scholarship casts doubts on these overstatements; scholars recognize today that the Townshend duties would have fallen far short of producing a sum even approaching the cost to Britain of administering the thirteen colonies, and that the revenue produced would have been less than one-tenth of that lost when the land tax in Great Britain was reduced one shilling. To ignore these truths is to admit both ignorance and provincialism, for not a textbook author ties to view the conflict over taxation from London rather than New York or Boston. One only compounds injury by listing as one of the Townshend Acts the Suspending Act which dissolved the New York Assembly; actually this was not a revenue measure and was passed at the insistence of the great friend of the colonists, William Pitt, Earl of Chatham, then head of the ministry.

The textbook story of resistance to the Townshend Acts is equally inflammatory and untruthful. One writer uses an obvious device to create an impression of impartiality; he has a mythical colonist speak as follows: 'Which of our rights will they try to take away next? What other unfair taxes will they impose upon us without our consent?' Young readers will forget that the speaker is a supposed colonist, and will only remember a despotic denial of 'rights' and 'unfair' taxes levied by George III and his ministers.

One episode in the record of resistance to the Townshend Acts—the so-called Boston Massacre—tempts every author of a

Junior High school text to raise high the banner of patriotism and let the chips of historical accuracy fall where they may (mixed metaphors come naturally after reading their purple prose). A typical version runs as follows:

> On the night of March 5, 1770, a crowd of men and boys were gathered on a Boston street. They had some difficulties with a soldier on guard duty. The boys threw snowballs at the man, and he shouted for help. Seven or eight other soldiers hurried out. Angry words followed. Suddenly the soldiers fired, and four men lay dead in the snow-covered street.

In that distorted account there is not a single hint of the truth: of the long record of insults and abuse suffered by the soldiers at the hands of Boston's inflamed citizenry, of the taunts of the mob that gathered, of the throwing of rocks and oyster shells, of the real threat to the troops' safety, of the probability that the shouted word 'Fire' came from the attackers rather than the attacked. No one can condone the shooting, but authors owe their readers an impartial explanation of its background. They also owe their audience an account of the events that followed: the arrest and trial of the soldiers, and their defence by John Adams and other prominent patriots. Certainly they should not imply, as one writer does, that the Massacre secured the repeal of the Townshend Acts: these measures were revoked by Parliament on the very day the attack took place.

Descriptions of the Tea Act in the Junior High school textbooks are relatively impartial, never deliberately wrong, and almost always misleading. The acts of colonial resistance that preceded this measure—the *Gaspée* affair and the organization by Samuel Adams of the Committees of Correspondence—receive but summary attention or are omitted entirely, even though they provide essential background. The Tea Act itself is described as a simple reduction of the tax on tea which would allow its sale at a lower price; no mention is made of its monopolistic features or of fears of American merchants that their profits from smuggling in Dutch tea would be endangered—two points essential in understanding upper-class colonial opposition. The measure may have been 'stupid' as one author labels it, and the British government may have 'made another foolish blunder' in naming Governor Thomas Hutchinson's sons as tea agents, but these judgments cannot compensate for failure to explain the complex economic situation responsible for the act. This was no hasty attempt to save a faltering East India Company at the colonies' expense, but a carefully planned measure understandable only in terms of the whole economy of empire.

The Boston Tea Party provides an obvious opportunity for rhetorical patriotism, and the textbook authors respond predictably. At least one gives the impression that American opposition was universal, and few pay proper attention to the role of merchants in organizing resistance for reasons that may not have been entirely patriotic. Against this background, the flag-waving accounts of Boston's tea party follow naturally. 'Then, on the night of December 16, the colonists acted,' reads one description. 'A band of Sons of Liberty, dressed as Indians, streamed down to the docks, shouting, "Boston Harbor a teapot this night!" As a crowd watched, they boarded the ships, ripped open the boxes of tea, and dumped the tea into the water.' This is an account notable for its precision, credibility, and apparent objectivity. But it omits far more than it says. Why the night of December 16? Were there no leaders? No organization and preliminary planning? Who dumped the tea? Who watched? Much is known about the Tea Party today that shows selfless loyalty to the patriot cause not to be the sole motive. Textbook authors owe their readers this side of the story if they are to earn the badge of objectivity.

The 'Intolerable Acts' which followed the Tea Party have long been separated by historians from the Quebec Act which happened to be passed by Parliament at the same time, but several textbook authors fail to make this distinction. Some make matters worse by failing to mention the laudable features of this measure—extending religious and legal relief to the French-Canadians of Quebec—while dwelling on the provisions that extended Quebec's boundaries into the Ohio Valley at the expense of other colonies' land claims there.

These mis-statements and distortions of Junior High school textbook authors not only create a biased picture of the chain of events leading to open colonial resistance, but they symbolize the utter failure of the writers to understand or convey an understanding of British colonial policy—what it was and what it was not. They often seem to feel that merely by using the abstraction 'mercantilism' and others like it they have accounted for colonial resistance. They do not realize that mercantilism was no single policy. By and large they emphasize only the 'bad' side of Britain's program, and neglect the hope of British statesmen to produce a stronger, more efficient empire. They neglect also the elementary fact of distance and the consequent impossibility of modifying policies in a short time; they overlook the necessity of British attention to many other parts of the world, foreign and colonial. They intrude twentieth-century judgments and stereotypes, and seem unaware that what would upset a citizen of 1965 would be meaningless to one of 1765, and that what we know so well was not known then. They homogenize colonial reactions so that not only do they often disregard the honest and sizeable group that remained loyal to the empire, but fail to appreciate the fact that Carolina frontiersmen, Tidewater planters, Philadelphia lawyers, and New England merchants responded quite differently to British policy. The causes of the American Revolution were complex, and any textbook writer worthy of his royalties should attempt to master them in their entirety before penning chapters that may distort the beliefs of a coming generation.

These generalizations are just as pertinent to the sections of the texts that describe the final steps toward revolution. The skirmishes at Lexington and Concord are a case in point. Despite the most searching scrutiny of every available source, historians today cannot state positively who fired the first shot at Lexington. Yet one textbook writer resolves the problem with a sweep of his pen. 'Minutemen,' he writes, 'faced them on the village green at Lexington, but did not attempt to stop their march. Nevertheless, the British fired upon the minutemen.' Another assigns guilt by innuendo: 'The British major orders the minutemen to scatter, but they stand their ground. A single shot rings out. Then a roar of fire comes from the British guns. Eight minutemen lie dead on the green at Lexington.' Still another makes his point by letting a nineteenth-century poet describe the battle:

> Yon voice that shouts, high-hoarse with ire,
> Fire!

The redcoats fire, the homespuns fall:
The homespuns' anxious voices call,
Brother, are hurt? and Where hit, John?
and Wipe this blood, and Men, come on
and Neighbor, do but lift thy head,
and Who is wounded? who is dead?
Seven are killed. My God! My God!
Seven lie dead on the village sod.

These may be stirring words, but they sadly distort the truth. So do the conclusions of another author who ascribes the accurate fire of the minutemen to their Indian fighting experiences (forgetting that there had been no hostile Indians in Eastern Massachusetts for a century), and seemingly takes pleasure in the fact that 273 British soldiers were killed on the march from Concord to Boston (the number, actually, both killed and wounded).

Perhaps the authors of Junior High school textbooks have not deliberately violated the canons of historical objectivity, but their treatment of the causes of the American Revolution certainly lays them open to such a charge. The impression that nearly all convey, even more persuasively than can be shown by quotations from their pages, is that the colonists were completely right and the British, although not consciously tyrannical, completely wrong. By repeatedly asserting American virtues, and by consistently labelling British measures as 'stupid' and products of 'the shortsighted, stubborn men who ruled the British Empire', they have reduced an unbelievably complex series of events into a simple contest between 'good' and 'bad', between 'hero' and 'villain'. This is not only untrue, but poor history.

To make matters worse, publishers of Junior High school textbooks bolster these prejudiced narratives with a multitude of 'teaching aids' that only compound the crime of bias. The following chart, taken from one, contains no mis-statements:

Colonial Opposition to British Actions	
British Action	Colonial Resistance
Proclamation of 1763	Violation of Proclamation provisions
Enforcement of Navigation and Trade Acts	Smuggling

Stamp Act, 1765	Stamp Act Congress; Refusal to buy Stamped Paper
Townshend Acts	Non-importation agreements
Tea tax retained after repeal of Townshend Acts, 1770	'Tea Parties'
Intolerable Acts	Training of minutemen
Destruction of colonial military supplies	Lexington and Concord

The impression created is of a series of British aggressions and American accommodation or resistance. History is never that simple, for man's behavioural patterns are too complex to be understandable in primitive cause and effect equations. Authors who deal in such elementary concepts are under-estimating their young readers no less than they are offending all principles of historical scholarship.

Not only charts, but illustrations and the inevitable questions that are clustered at the end of every textbook chapter lend themselves to the furtherance of prejudice. No impartial historian would use a contemporary propaganda drawing of the Boston Massacre to illustrate that event, but one textbook publisher is guilty of that device. Similarly, questions on 'Why did the colonists begin to resist British laws?' and 'Explain how the people of Boston were punished by the Intolerable Acts' are hardly representative of both sides of the story. In their educational aids, as in many of their textual statements, the textbooks used in Junior High schools stray far from an objective and impartial statement of the causes of the American Revolution.

(b) *Course of the American Revolution*

In fairness to the authors and publishers of Junior High school texts, it must be said that most have entitled their chapters dealing with the military history of the Revolutionary War to emphasize 'independence' rather than the more subjective concept of 'freedom'. Only one violates this rule with the words 'THE COLONIES WIN THEIR FREEDOM'. Yet the accounts of the war that parade under this impartial banner are themselves largely partial; rare is the author who can resist painting the Americans in heroes' garb and the British in the gaudy garments of villainy. No less deplorable is the tendency of all

39

writers to overemphasize some battles and underemphasize others, creating an impression of an unbroken series of American victories and British losses. Most, too, reveal a regrettable tendency to deny America's allies their proper credit for the eventual victory.

Most texts begin their story with a heroic account of Ethan Allen's attacks on Forts Ticonderoga and Crown Point, marred by the repetition of the oft-discredited cliché that Allen demanded Ticonderoga's surrender 'in the name of the Great Jehovah and the Continental Congress'. Some apparently realize that they are repeating an untruth, but sink to the use of such devices as 'Allen was said to have shouted', or 'it is reported that he cried'. Untruths should be omitted, not paraded as rumour which might be believed by the reader.

Similarly, in describing the Battle of Bunker Hill, authors show themselves sufficiently abreast of modern scholarship to mention Breed's Hill, but still purple their prose with comments about 'bold Americans' and 'sharpshooting Americans' who left 'dead and dying redcoats' covering the hillside before running out of powder. Again they write no untruths, but the impression of heroic colonists overwhelming a superior enemy persists; a reader has to remind himself that the Americans actually lost. Contrast these distortions with the simple statement of another textbook writer at this level: 'On June 17 American troops clashed with the British on Breed's Hill in Charlestown, Massachusetts, and gave way only on the third assault.' Less glamorous, perhaps, but also less guilty of stirring anti-British prejudices.

The Declaration of Independence is properly recognized as a landmark not only in the history of the Revolution but in the history of liberty, but the events leading to this immortal document are less accurately depicted. Thomas Paine's *Common Sense* usually receives the acclaim that it deserves, but one author overgilds the lily by adding that 'he knew much of British tyranny which had forced him to leave England'; actually Paine left his homeland when he was discharged from the excise service for writing a pamphlet urging more pay for excisemen. Seldom do textbooks at the Junior High school level sufficiently stress the international purposes of the Declaration as a device to win French aid or the fact that its sentiments as well as its language were English. Too few point out that a large minority of Englishmen subscribed to its general principles; too many parade its recital of the sins of George III as evidences of fact rather than as instruments of propaganda. Nor is the cause of accuracy aided by one author who cites George III's approval of General Gage's belief that the colonists would 'be lions whilst we are lambs, but if we take the resolute part they will undoubtedly prove very meek'. Gage made that remark to the King in March, 1773, not in 1776 as the writer implies.

The hiring of Hessian troops by Britain in the months following the outbreak of hostilities offers textbook authors another opportunity to demonstrate the heartlessness of George III. No text even hints at the prevalence of this practice in the eighteenth century, or suggests that hired soldiers were somewhat less capable fighters than the British regulars. Instead one damns the Hessian as 'a hired fighter without loyalty to any cause' (conjuring up a hostile image to twentieth-century youths whose conception of loyalty differs from that of the eighteenth century), and another adds that 'it was bad enough to have British redcoats swaggering up and down their streets' without having the king hire German soldiers. How, one might ask timidly, did that author know that English troops 'swaggered?'

George Washington's generalship in the early years of the Revolution offers writers an opportunity to gloss over errors and magnify victories. The unsuccessful invasion of Canada receives but scant notice, and not a single textbook questions the wisdom of launching a winter campaign against Quebec. Historians agree that General Howe lost an opportunity to scatter the rebel forces after Washington's defeat at the Battle of Long Island; authors of texts barely mention the defeat and one translates Howe's 'lost opportunity' into his failure to pursue the Americans across the Delaware River. The colonists' failures at Brooklyn Heights and on Manhattan Island are either not mentioned or are glossed over by most authors; one goes so far as to suggest that Howe's return to New York during the winter of 1776 was due to his love of good living rather than his knowledge of the hazards of winter campaigning. General Howe was not a shining example of British military genius, but historians today recognize that most of his moves were dictated by a sound knowledge of strategy as understood at that time.

More to the taste of textbook writers is the American victory at the Battle of Saratoga, but most seem so woefully ignorant of what really happened there that the results are disastrous. Thus (to cite but a few inaccuracies), Howe was not in New Jersey at the start of the campaign; Burgoyne's army was not 'huge' but was actually outnumbered by Gates' opposition force; the British did recapture Forts Ticonderoga and Crown Point; Gates was in command of the American army, not General Philip Schuyler. More, damaging to the truth is the belief of some authors that Burgoyne was properly instructed by his superiors and should bear the whole burden of defeat; we know instead that the failure of Germain and Howe to send him proper orders was a contributory cause to his downfall. Carelessness with the findings of recent scholarship rather than superpatriotism seems the besetting sin of textbook authors when trying to interpret the Battle of Saratoga.

The southern and western campaigns at the close of the Revolution also offer an opportunity to underemphasize American defeats and overemphasize American victories. General Gates' conduct at the Battle of Camden is seldom mentioned, nor is his replacement by General Greene deemed worthy of inclusion. One author at least tells his readers that all of Georgia, the Carolinas, and southern Virginia fell to the British, without reminding them that the patriots regained control as soon as Cornwallis' army moved on; that general arrived at Yorktown beset by the constant menace of reprisal attacks from the rear, not as the master of a conquered southland. When dealing with the western campaigns, textbook authors almost universally brand Captain Hamilton of Detroit as a 'hair-buyer' who incited the Indians and award George Rogers Clark the glory of winning the Old Northwest for the United States. Actually Hamilton bought not a single scalp and incited not a single red man, while Clark's victories at Kaskaskia and Vincennes were spectacular but did not assure the West for the new nation; this was actually a gift from the far-sighted Lord Shelburne at the peace table.

The war at sea, although but slightly mentioned by the majority of textbook authors, is consistently misunderstood.

Not a single writer who deals with the subject can resist describing John Paul Jones' victory over the *Serapis*, but all are strangely silent on the chain of English triumphs that drove the American navy from the seas.

These accounts of the military engagements of the Revolution are usually not consciously biased, but their total effect is to create an impression of a righteous victory of the 'good guys' over the 'bad guys'. This is accomplished by overstressing American triumphs and understressing defeats, by a subtle employment of adjectives that picture the colonists as superior and the British as inferior, and by a compounding of minor errors to picture the angels as even more godlike and the devils as even more satanic than the truth allows. Against such a background the authors are able to describe the peace negotiations as a logical and simple aftermath of an overwhelming triumph for righteousness. This is particularly unfortunate, for the accounts almost universally fail to mention the complex divisions among the allies which were far more responsible for the nature of the Treaty of Paris than the 'able diplomats' who are given credit for wresting a generous settlement from a beaten foe. Perhaps the manipulations of the American, French, Spanish, and British statesmen are too intricate to be inflicted in detail on the young, but there is still no justification for an account of the peace settlement that fails to mention that the war did not end at Yorktown, that omits a single word about the role of France and Spain, and that ascribes the favourable result solely to the fact that John Adams, John Jay, and Benjamin Franklin 'worked carefully and slowly—so slowly that nearly two years passed before the treaty was completed'.

In their discussions of both the origins and course of the American Revolution, authors of Junior High school textbooks stand indicted for nationalistic bias, seldom openly expressed, but so consistently present through emphasis and nuance that the result is the same. In each of the widely circulated texts the cumulative impact of minor mis-statements or one-sided descriptions reveals a subconscious assumption of American superiority. The author who mentions not a single American defeat save that at Bunker Hill—and then suggests that this was a moral victory—is only guilty of exaggerating prejudices present in all. The result is unfortunate. Youthful readers will gain an impression of American virtue and British sin that does not accord with the facts. Moreover, they will retain the impression that the happy outcome of the war for the United States was due entirely to the 'brilliant' leadership of its generals, and not to the generous aid furnished by France and Spain, the generosity of the British peace commissioners, and the questionable conduct of the American negotiators in deserting their allies. Fairness, no less than historical accuracy, demands that this story of the nation's origins be displaced for one nearer the truth.

2. AMERICAN HIGH SCHOOL TEXTBOOKS[1]

Those who search for evidence of nationalistic bias in the more advanced textbooks used in the High schools of the United States will be less richly rewarded than those who confine themselves to the Junior High school books. That the latter should succumb more completely to prejudice is easily understandable. The Junior High school text is designed for students with a lower comprehension level, encouraging the author to oversimplify complexities and to stress the myths that seemingly have greater appeal to the young. Senior High school textbooks, on the other hand, can indulge in more subtleties. They are allowed greater space for fuller explanations and are designed to attract a more mature audience than one that would be impressed with the legends that encrust the truth in every nation's history. For these reasons, evidences of overt bias are largely lacking, and examples of subconscious bias and group superiority are less flagrant.

Yet bias does exist; not a single textbook among those most widely used in American high schools is free of mis-statement, questionable word choice, nuances of language, the cumulative presentation of evidence in a manner favouring one side or another, and the selection of facts that glorify America at the expense of Britain. The result is a fabric of half-truths that must have an adverse effect on a proper understanding of the British and American past.

[1] For a list of High school textbooks analysed and cited in this section, see Preface, p. xii.

The American Revolution

(a) *Causes of the American Revolution*

Fortunately the authors of High school textbooks are able
to include adequate discussions of such measures as the Sugar
Act and Currency Act (including the forces behind them)
which are omitted with such disastrous results from lower-level
books. Nor do they feel required to cater to immature minds by
retelling discredited tales of Patrick Henry and Ethan Allen
through the dubious device of 'it is said that'. For the most part
they tell a straightforward honest story of the Revolution; bias
intrudes largely through the selection of events to emphasize,
subconscious nuances in language, and unfamiliarity with
modern historical interpretation. Yet one basic fault remains:
all textbooks view the happenings of 1763–1776 through
American spectacles; Britain is seen only dimly and distantly
with little appreciation for her problems and little explanation
of her policies. The author able to stand simultaneously in
London and New York has not yet written a High school text.

Most writers on this level sympathize with Britain's reasons
for inaugurating the policies that led to Revolution, but a few
show their misunderstanding. Thus one reveals that he is out of
step with recent scholarship by saying that British statesmen
favoured new revenue measures so that 'the Americans should
be made to pay their share of the immense cost of the Seven
Years' War'; actually the laws were designed to allow the
colonies to pay a portion of the expenses of frontier defence, not
past debts. This same confusion exists in the mind of another
textbook author who believes that to British ministers seeking
means of reducing their nation's large war debt 'the remedy
appeared to be obvious: raise more money in the colonies'.

These wanderings from the path of truth are less alarming
than the general failure of text writers to appreciate what a
leading historian has called 'the imperial problem'. England,
freed in 1763 from the need of defending her colonies against
France, was abruptly confronted with the task of organizing her
vast empire economically and politically. The revisions in policy
that resulted were not directed solely against the Americas, as
the locally oriented historians of the past believed. This should
be explained, as should the habits of independence that had,
through usage, come to be considered rights by the colonists.
When a textbook author ascribes colonial resentment to being

'dictated to by a minister in London who had little understanding of their problems' he might have added with equal
truth that the colonists had no more understanding of Britain's
complex problems. No pupil can gain an accurate impression
of these problems without some instruction in Britain's financial
situation, yet this is customarily lacking from texts. To tell
readers, as does one author, that the shift in England's policy
after 1763 was owing to a desire 'to curtail the growing tendency toward self-government in the colonies' is to pervert the
truth.

Almost equally regrettable is the proneness of writers to
perpetuate careless errors in their discussions of the origins of
Britain's new policies after 1763. A majority fail to make clear
the temporary nature of the Proclamation Line of 1763. Most
describe the plan to send ten thousand troops to America without linking that decision with Pontiac's Rebellion and the need
for border defence; only one notes that many of the soldiers
were destined for the British West Indies. Although all mention
the Sugar and Currency Acts of 1764, most fail to explain the
reasons for these measures; no one can appreciate England's
desire for the latter Act without awareness of the quantity of
paper currency issued by the colonies and used in depreciated
form to pay debts to London merchants. Nor can pupils understand the operation of the Sugar Act without knowing that it
cut duties by half and still left the Americans free to buy their
molasses from the British West Indies. Even the one author
who correctly states that the levy was halved damns it a page
later as 'high'.

Few textbook writers seem willing—or able—to enlighten
pupils on the broad economic problems that faced Britain in the
reconstruction of her empire, preferring instead to imply that
each act was aimed exclusively at the thirteen American
colonies and totally omitting the historic setting of British policy.
A case in point is the use of writs of assistance in the enforce-
ment of revenue and trade measures. These had long been used
in England, and had been introduced into America during the
Seven Years' War in an attempt to check colonial trade with
the enemy. Yet textbooks seem to stress, as historians did a half-
century ago, that the writs were inflicted on the colonists after
1763 in a desperate effort to enforce the Navigation Acts.

Modern scholars have also demonstrated that colonial smuggling was far less common than previously assumed, yet this nugget of information has escaped the textbook writers. At least one is similarly guilty of misrepresenting the Woollen, Hat, and Iron acts by painting a grim picture of the devastation they would have created if enforced, rather than mentioning that crown officials made no attempt to apply sections of the measures harmful to the economy.

Authors seem equally incapable of resisting the temptation to paint the British characters in the Revolutionary drama with a tar brush. Although scholars have relegated the old image of George III as an ambitious tyrant to the historical ash-can, some texts repeat the story of his mother's statement, 'George, be a King', and two picture him as the sole architect of the policies that stirred American resentment. 'He was,' says one author 'determined to rule as well as sit on the throne. Hence he chose ministers who were ready to do his bidding.' That this viewpoint grossly exaggerates George's role as a policy maker is well known to historians who see England's actions as a response on the part of administrators to pressing imperial problems. George's ministers fare little better than their ruler. Grenville to one text writer was a 'narrow-minded' man who 'could not grasp the colonial point of view'; to another he was an 'obstinate and autocratic man' who 'turned a deaf ear to colonial protests'; to still another a 'conscientious, narrow-minded man, who was determined to make the American colonies realize their obligations to the empire'. If authors had used the space devoted to these epithets to explain the English political factions and to emphasize that the administration of the whole empire chiefly concerned Grenville, their narratives would be both fairer and more accurate.

Senior High school texts generally describe the two measures that stirred the greatest protest—the Stamp Act and the Townshend Acts—with a commendable attempt at objectivity, but some curious omissions and distortions still survive. Few authors state, for example, that Grenville gave the colonists an opportunity to propose an alternative to the Stamp Act, or bother to describe the English tax structure of that day to show that taxpayers there paid a similar tax at an even higher rate. If a writer describes the American taxes as 'burdensome', what term might he have used had he pictured the English scene?

The Townshend Act is similarly distorted at the hands of some authors of High school textbooks. Descriptions of the financial situation within Britain that made these measures necessary are normally omitted; that omission might have been repaired if writers had not used their space to describe Charles Townshend as 'Champagne Charley' and recount that he was 'a brilliant orator when under the influence of liquor'—information of precious little significance, even if true. Nor is the cause of accuracy advanced when an author quotes Townshend as dismissing colonial opposition to the measures as 'so much nonsense' when what he actually said was: 'I do not know any distinction between internal and external taxes; it is a distinction without a difference; it is perfect nonsense.' The truth is that Townshend realized his duties would not raise one-tenth of the revenue lost when the land tax in Britain was reduced twenty-five per cent, but believed that such a measure was needed to convince English taxpayers that the colonists were making some contribution, no matter how small, to the support of the empire. This was his motivation, not a sudden whim or vindictiveness against the Americans, as some textbooks suggest.

Just as senior High school textbooks describe colonial opposition to the Stamp Act and Townshend Duties on a distinctly less partisan plane than those used in the lower grades, so other incidents are related more objectively. None, for example, commits the crime of depicting the Boston Massacre as seen through Paul Revere's propaganda cartoon; when this is used as an illustration it is usually properly identified. Yet there is much room for improvement. Some overstress the role of the non-importation agreements in affecting repeal of the measures, suggesting a triumph for American initiative. Some endow the colonists with too much determination; to say that they were "too powerful, too mature, too skilled, and too experienced to be considered pawns, subject to the whims of British policy', is to read the future into the past. In this area of discussion, as in many others, the authors do not attempt to understand and appreciate the British situation and attitudes. They stand firmly in Boston or Williamsburg rather than in London. If they aspired to a trans-Atlantic viewpoint, they would not describe the Boston Massacre so one-sidedly, and

EVENTS LEADING TO THE AMERICAN REVOLUTION

	BRITISH ACTION	COLONIAL REACTION
1733	Molasses Act passed	Smuggling became widespread
1750	Manufacture of ironware forbidden	
1763	Proclamation of 1763 closed frontier	Not obeyed
1764	Sugar Act, Currency Act passed	
1765	Quartering Act, Stamp Act passed	Sons of Liberty destroyed stamps
		Stamp Act Congress
		Nonimportation agreement
1766	Stamp Act repealed	Rejoicing in colonies
1767	Townshend Acts; new efforts to stop smuggling	Nonimportation revived; customs officers' attacked by mobs
1768	British troops sent to Boston	Massachusetts' Circular Letter to other colonies
		Pestering of troops; Boston Massacre, 1770
1770	Repeal of Townshend duties except tax on tea	Burning of the customs schooner *Gaspée*, 1772
	Quartering Act expired	Committees of correspondence active
1773	Tea Act passed	Tea ships not allowed to unload
		Boston Tea Party
1774	Intolerable Acts	First Continental Congress met
1775	American ports closed	Lexington and Concord, April 1775
		Second Continental Congress convened May 2
		Washington appointed commander in chief
		Battle of Bunker Hill, June 17
		Common Sense published, January
1776	Siege of Boston	Declaration of Independence, July 4, 1776
	British evacuated Boston and occupied New York	

3. Chart from an American High School textbook showing the cause-and-affect relationship between British acts of 'aggression' and colonial 'adjustment'. The dangers of over-compression are also revealed in such phrases as 'Proclamation of 1763 closed frontier'.

4. Paul Revere's propaganda cartoon of the Boston Massacre, reproduced in an American Junior High School textbook with a caption suggesting that the event itself was accurately pictured.

5. An imaginative version of the Boston Massacre, in which British troops fire on 'unarmed colonists'. This picture is used in a popular American Junior High School textbook.

would surely mention that the English soldiers charged with the killings were defended by John Adams and Josiah Quincy. Similarly they would not state, as does one author, that the troops were shifted to the interior after the Massacre; actually they were withdrawn to islands in Boston Harbour.

Accounts of the final period of misunderstanding between 1773 and 1776 are also characterized by an obvious attempt at objectivity, but none the less there emerges an identical bias stemming from an inadequate comprehension of the British scene or viewpoint. Although properly mentioned in most textbooks, the *Gaspée* affair does not appear in all. More serious is the failure to explain that the transfer of trials to England after this episode brought to a climax a long period in which American juries demonstrated their consistent unwillingness to convict in smuggling cases, despite the overwhelming weight of evidence. Nor does any author relate that Admiralty Courts in Britain had always functioned under civil law without jury trials, again a lack of historical setting.

There is a general tendency at this point in the story for authors to refer to 'blunders' of the ministry and to 'British tyranny'—judgments mirroring colonial rather than mother-country attitudes. They also accept unquestioningly the viewpoint of colonial radicals that 'taxation without representation' violated the fundamental rights of colonists as Englishmen. Actually the Americans were determined to resist taxation by Parliament with or without representation, as they revealed when they refused to consider offers of representation. Their actions suggest that they took their stand only because they knew themselves to be less burdened by taxes than the people of the homeland, and that the constitutional arguments they advanced only rationalized economic motives.

The tendency of textbook writers to accept unquestioningly the colonial viewpoint becomes even clearer as they deal with the Boston Tea Party and Britain's punitive measures. In some cases the Tea Act is described without mentioning two essential facts: opposition to the measure was led by merchants and shopkeepers who could no longer profit from selling smuggled tea, and the act was passed by Parliament not merely to rescue a badly administered East India Company but for its effects on the entire British economy. One text commits the unpardonable sin of failing to mention that the measure lowered rather than raised the price of tea and that the English consumer would henceforth be required to pay twice as much as the American; another draws the remarkable conclusion that the act was passed only because members of Parliament 'owned stock in the company'. Several authors explain colonial opposition on the grounds that the creation of one monopoly would encourage others; one even adds gratuitously that 'this latest British Act seemed to threaten all free enterprise'. These judgments ignore the fact that Parliament viewed the act as a temporary measure, that England was even more fully committed to capitalism than America, and that precedents for this type of economic rehabilitation existed in ample numbers.

The Intolerable Acts are properly presented as justified in most High school textbooks, but again authors show a tendency to view these laws from a local rather than an imperial vantage point. The name assigned them reveals this; 'Intolerable Acts' was the derogatory label fastened on them by the Americans, while in Britain they were known as the Restraining Acts or the Coercion Acts. Even more misleading—and surprising—is the number of writers who link the Quebec Act with the Intolerable Acts; actually the former had been drafted before the Tea Party. Some compound this injustice by branding the measures as 'far too extreme' or by commenting that 'the British had clumsily stepped hard on the toes' of Boston merchants. Such a judgment reveals a colonial bias as well as a failure to understand England's problem; surely an act of rebellion such as that committed in Boston would be followed by retaliation in any country of the world, then and now. One author can be charged with gross carelessness as well as prejudice for including a John Singleton Copley portrait of Samuel Adams which 'seems to show him pointing disdainfully at some new evidence of British despotism' when actually the picture shows Adams pointing with pride to the Massachusetts charter!

Personalities are viewed by most textbook writers through the eyes of colonial contemporaries, with little attempt to place them in their proper historical setting. Perhaps it is accurate to say that George III 'used this power of patronage to bribe members of Parliament', but the American student should also be told that 'influence' of this sort was commonplace in the eighteenth century, that the patronage system was necessary because no political parties existed and both Government and Opposition could operate only by recruiting votes in this way, and that the monarch's authority was limited. Modern British historians would use less weighted words than 'favouritism' and 'bribery' in describing George's reign, and would qualify their remarks by defining 'bribery' as the term was understood at the time. To ascribe British defeat in the Revolution partly to these factors, as one author does, is to ignore the fact that there was just as much 'favouritism and bribery' in England in the years of victory between 1756 and 1763, and just as much 'influence' in colonial Virginia.

Subconscious national bias also seems to warp the viewpoint of authors as they describe the battles of Lexington and Concord. None makes the mistake of pronouncing that the first shot was fired by British troops, but to say that it came from an 'unknown soldier' and that this was a 'signal' for a British volley is to leave the impression that the soldier was British. So also does the statement that the minutemen 'waited for the British and tried to halt them. But the British soldiers routed the minutemen easily, and leaving eight colonists dead or dying at Lexington, they pushed on the Concord'. An immature American reader could only conclude that British guns had cut down the peaceful colonists. This same prejudice by innuendo mars the accounts of the British retreat to Boston. Remarks about the 'deadly fire' and 'deadly accuracy' of the minutemen contradict the findings of modern historians: that only one bullet of every three hundred fired by the patriots found its mark. Even the most impartial accounts of this engagement exaggerate the American success by listing only the British losses without telling the number involved or the American casualties.

These deliberate or subconscious alterations of the facts of history to fit the preconceived nationalistic attitudes of the author typify the story of the causes of the Revolution found in the High school textbooks of today. Overt bias is almost completely lacking; each writer is obviously seeking objectivity within his own limited capacities to achieve that goal. They fail for two basic reasons. One is their unfamiliarity with the findings of present-day scholarship, particularly in the field of

British history which paints both the leaders and politics of that day in a more understandable rôle. The other is the inability of authors to divorce themselves from the American viewpoint; they subconsciously associate themselves with the rebellious colonists, and see events through rebel eyes. National history will never be free of bias until authors master the art of international thinking. They can do this only by consciously erasing the memory of their heritage, with all its cluster of myth and legend, and by immersing themselves so completely in the historical literature of both nations that the values and viewpoint of each become tools for everyday use. Nor will authors achieve objectivity until they cast off present-mindedness and view developments in their historical context. These are difficult assignments, but worthy of the effort if non-biased history is the result.

(b) *Course of the American Revolution*

A higher level of reader sophistication allows High school textbook authors to deal with the military and diplomatic events of the Revolutionary era more accurately and objectively than in books designed for Junior High school classes. They are able to explain victories and defeats to some degree rather than merely ascribing them to the incompetence of British generals, the ineffectiveness of troops unwilling to fight in Indian fashion, and the superior marksmanship of the American sharpshooters. The result is a reasonably acceptable picture of the war in most textbooks, although there are notable exceptions. Those who fail in their assignments are either subconsciously biased or unaware of the findings of recent scholarship. One or two authors seem in addition unbelievably careless, committing unpardonable blunders with facts which can charitably be blamed only on hasty composition.

Typical of the annoying distortions usual in the High school texts is their treatment of the Hessians. These hired troops are not indeed pictured as ogres whose employment revealed the brutality of George III, yet in not a single instance is the fact stressed that mercenary soldiers were commonly used by all powers in the eighteenth century. Similarly, authors reflect modern views in describing the Loyalists not as rabble but as the cultural élite of colonial America, but some go so far in this direction that they obscure the fact that many back-country small-farmers were Tories, as were most Methodists in all walks of life. One errs in allotting half the population to the Loyalist cause; one-third is a more accurate figure.

Minor evidences of bias intrude in the descriptions of the first skirmishes of the war. Only rarely do textbooks point out the American error in launching the Quebec campaign, or explain the failure of the French-Canadians to rally to the patriot cause by pointing out the ethnic and religious bigotry of the New Englanders. The capture of Fort Ticonderoga is normally described without inflicting the 'Great Jehovah and Continental Congress' legend on the reader, but no author ascribes Ethan Allen's easy victory to the fact that the fort had decayed until it was hardly defensible and the even more telling fact that its fifty defenders did not know war had been declared. In the same vein American troops at Bunker Hill are praised for their valiant stand in some textbooks, but no similar pat on the back is awarded the British attackers who twice charged up the hill carrying full packs. Colonial defeat on this occasion is usually ascribed to exhaustion of the power supply.

The adoption of the Declaration of Independence allows authors to reveal both the depth and extent of their sub-conscious acceptance of the American stand as right and just. Few attempt to explain that this was a practical document as well as a philosophical justification for independence; its emphasis on natural rights was designed to attract French aid, just as its stress on the absolutism of George III was aimed at solidifying support from colonial patriots. Mention of these realistic points does not detract from the idealism of its framers, or dim the importance of its message. Textbook authors are also guilty of accepting the Declaration's charges that George III was a tyrant and American liberties endangered. This is understandable; that document has become such a symbol of democratic thought that authors tend to overlook its propaganda character. To believe all its charges is as far-fetched as to expect the circus to be the marvel described on the posters. Authors must curb this temptation if they are to reveal the Declaration of Independence for what it was in the eighteenth century, not the twentieth. They should also resist the temptation to quote Thomas Paine's *Common Sense* as the gospel truth

53

rather than as the emotion-charged propaganda that it was; one who adds Washington's endorsement of Paine's 'sound doctrine and unanswerable reasoning' goes even further in parading fiction as truth.

In discussing the battles of the Revolution, authors of High school textbooks manifest the same faults that mar those used on lower levels, although less blatantly. They tend to overstress American victories and understress American defeats; readers emerge with the impression that the patriots lost only the Battle of Bunker Hill during the war, and this only because they ran out of powder. Washington's defeat at Brooklyn Heights is either not mentioned or is characterized as part of the 'miracle of strategy' by which he accomplished his 'masterly retreat across the East River'. No author criticizes Washington for placing his army on an island surrounded by waters dominated by the British navy, or explains that the Howe brothers hesitated to follow up their victory because they hoped to end the war by negotiation. Nor is Washington condemned for the loss of forts Washington and Lee in the New York campaign, even in the rare instances when those events are mentioned. By contrast, his victories at Trenton and Princeton brought to a climax a 'brilliant campaign' which forced the British to 'fall back in panic'. One author even joins Frederick the Great in labelling this 'one of the most brilliant [campaigns] in military history'; another is guilty of comparable exaggeration when he writes that they 'recovered most of the state of New Jersey'. Washington's exploits at this time need no gilding.

Later military events are explained with equal partiality. General Howe is berated in one textbook for his 'blunder in not co-operating with Burgoyne', even though the authors had earlier pointed out that the 'pleasure-loving Germain' had forgotten to send him his orders. Few textbooks mirror the modern historical opinion that Burgoyne, Germain, and Howe were equally to blame for the loss at Saratoga, and that difficulties in overseas communication was a major cause of the defeat. Descriptions of the southen campaigns also are distorted to stress American successes. One author writes that the American victory at King's Mountain 'struck terror into Cornwallis' army', that Morgan's victory at Cowpens was 'brilliant', and that Cornwallis was frustrated by 'the superior strategy of his opponents'. Colonial losses at Charleston, Camden and Guilford Court House are usually forgotten, but space is found for descriptions of the British 'plundering and terrorizing the Patriots'. The image that emerges of events leading to Yorktown is one of repeated American victories, the steady retreat of red-coated marauders, and the vast superiority of colonial fighters.

Yorktown itself fares little better. To deal objectively with this battle, authors should make two things clear: first that Washington's victory would have been impossible without French naval aid, and second that the American land force not only outnumbered the British but was reinforced by French soldiers and officers. Modern scholars have determined that about 8,845 colonial and 7,800 French soldiers opposed 6,000 British. This easily available information appears but seldom in textbook accounts of the battle. Only patriotic enthusiasm —or colossal ignorance—could inspire an author to say, as one does, that Yorktown was 'the most significant defeat in the history of the British Empire', and only lack of historical good sense could allow nearly all writers to suggest that the Revolution ended with this battle.

Nothing was further from the truth. Two large British armies remained in the country, while the year 1782 was to unfold a whole series of dramatic events in the world-wide conflict. Yet not a single textbook mentions such an important development as Dunning's motion in Parliament and the fall of Lord North's government. Not one stresses the now understood fact that the war had become extremely unpopular in England. These omissions cloud the discussions of the peace negotiations, which are further marred by repetition of the disproven claim that George Rogers Clark won the West. One author goes beyond this distortion to suggest that England was willing to give the Americans lands west of the Appalachians 'to bribe us out of the war'. These summary statements deny Lord Shelburne the credit due him for recognizing the needs of an expanding population if the United States was to live in peace with the rest of the world.

High school textbooks, slightly less than those used in Junior High schools, stand indicted for a number of crimes against impartiality, even though little overt bias mars their pages.

Their authors view events through American eyes; to them George Washington is such an obvious hero that his enemies must automatically be wrong. This leads to an overemphasis on patriot victories and a convenient omission of patriot defeats; even the sea battles are described as the *Bonhomme Richard's* triumph over the *Serapis* and John Paul Jones' 'three hundred' captured prizes with never a mention of the English successes that drove the small American navy from the seas.

Equally to be deplored is the textbook authors' tendency to minimize, although to be sure never to ignore, the contributions to independence made by France, and to overlook entirely the extent of European hostility to Great Britain. No less unfortunate is their tendency to suggest that certain evil practices were the monopoly of England: the British used mercenaries and Indians while the colonists did not; the British plundered and ravaged the countryside while the Americans were guilty of no such crimes. Once more the authors cannot be convicted of mis-statement, only a suspicious memory failure when the time arrives to describe American attempts—largely unsuccessful—to recruit Indian allies, or the mobs that harassed the Loyalists. These faults, compounded by a lack of knowledge of the Britain of that day, have created textbook accounts of the Revolution that cannot stand the test of objectivity, and that contribute to the shaping of a distorted image of Great Britain in the minds of impressionable readers.

3. BRITISH SECONDARY SCHOOL TEXTBOOKS[1]

Identical standards employed in detecting nationalistic bias in American Junior High school and High school history textbooks cannot be used in appraising those written in England and Wales. This is true for several reasons. First, the use and purpose of the textbook varies between the two educational systems; the English version is designed to teach rather than popularize and is used by instructors sufficiently versed in their subjects that they can provide the major interpretations necessary. Second, the vast time span of British history, in contrast with that of the United States, forces textbook authors to

[1] A list of English textbooks used in this appraisal will be found in the Preface, pp. xii–xiii.

minimize or ignore events of less than major importance; books covering more than a thousand years of history will necessarily have comparatively little space for the American Revolution and much less for such a minor event as the War of 1812. Third, tradition in Britain focuses attention on the earlier eras, with a corresponding lack of emphasis on the later period favoured in American education; consequently English texts devote less space to the nineteenth century. Finally, the age and educational levels of those using British textbooks varies so greatly from their more standardized American counterparts that an exact comparison seems impossible; some English books seem to assume far more sophisticated readers than American volumes, and others less sophisticated readers.

The space limitations imposed on English textbook writers by the nature of their assignment decree that the American Revolution receives but scant treatment. The result illustrates abundantly 'bias by omission'; in compressing their accounts into a few paragraphs, the authors deal almost exclusively with the issue of taxation as a cause, and reveal little awareness of the many complex forces that drove the colonists to rebellion. By omitting mention of the idealism of the people and the justice of many of their arguments, the authors paint a distorted picture, one that can be remedied only by a change in proportions.

As if to compensate for their inability to present the American cause fully, many English authors seem to lean over backwards to avoid any impression of national bias. The result might be termed 'bias in reverse'. Some go out of their way to berate Britain for the colonies' troubles, even to the degree of saddling George III with most of the blame—a judgment scarcely expected for their knowledge of English history would reveal the error of such a view. The colonists, by contrast, are showered with praise so lavish as to be almost ludicrous; to recognize George Washington as an able leader is one thing, but to label him 'unbeatable' and say that he was 'perhaps the greatest' of all Americans is gilding the lily. Such exaggeration might well create attitudes in the minds of English schoolboys as hostile to the United States as overt bias. The simple truths of history are, in the long run, more telling than the most extravagant distortions.

Authors in England and Wales are also guilty of unpardonable ignorance of American history and geography, just as American authors are woefully uninformed on the state of British politics during the Revolutionary era. More homework is clearly essential for both. When an author says that all colonies had royal governors, that Congress met at Philadelphia while Washington was at Valley Forge, and that Yorktown is in North Carolina, he reveals gaps in his knowledge that lessen confidence in his judgment.

Similar examples—many of them illustrating ignorance of the elementary facts of British history as well as American—can be summoned in alarming number: the French retained Louisiana in 1763; British possessions in America were twenty times larger after 1763 than before 1754; southern colonies were generally loyal while the northern solidly opposed Britain; troops were sent to America to guard the colonists from the French rather than the Indians; brewers were the most important group injured by the Stamp Act; the Townshend Acts were passed in 1768; feeling against England ran riot for three years after the repeal of the Townshend Duties; the colonists began to fight immediately after the passage of the Intolerable Acts; British casualties on April 19, 1775, totalled sixty-five men; Thomas Paine was exiled to America; the American flag was copied from the East India Company flag; Burgoyne surrendered on October 17 (not October 7) to an army made up entirely of local militia; Cornwallis overran Pennsylvania; George Washington spent the winter of 1776–1777 at Valley Forge; Yorktown is on the James River; Lafayette was at New York holding back Clinton rather than at Yorktown harassing Cornwallis; Cornwallis' surrender ended the war; the first congress under the Constitution met in 1788; West Point has since the Revolution been the 'key' fortress guarding the northern states. Such inexcusable factual errors as these, found in virtually every English textbook examined, prevent pupils from obtaining a clear and unbiased picture of the past. Indeed, they make impossible the forming of any sensible view of what, so far as historians can know, really happened.

These points can be brought home by a more detailed examination of the sins of the textbook writers of England and Wales, looking especially at the three areas where their practices are most questionable: their errors of omission, their occasional indulgence in open or subconscious bias, and their 'bias in reverse'.

(a) *Errors of Omission*

Current practice in English education is to allot more time to the American Revolution and, for that matter, more time to American history in general, than has been the custom in the past; criticisms levied against textbooks for scant mention of the War for Independence applies principally to older books, or to those that have been inadequately revised in recent editions. It is hoped that the committee's criticisms will encourage this trend towards greater emphasis on American history.

Certainly no pupil can understand the Revolution if he must gain his knowledge from one paragraph or even half a dozen small pages. When one considers that even in the Revolutionary age—since we must avoid wisdom after the fact —Englishmen of different interests and backgrounds recognized that America might one day become the seat of the British Empire, one must believe that its creation deserves a fuller treatment than this:

> The Americans (as we shall now begin to call the British colonists in North America) had for a long time objected to being ruled from London and to having little to say in their own most important affairs. Now that they no longer feared conquest by the French they began to quarrel very seriously with the British government. The British government made little attempt to understand their point of view, so in 1776 they declared themselves independent states. The British government sent an army to bring them back to obedience. But France and Spain, longing for revenge on Britain for their defeat in 1763, came to the colonists' aid. By 1783 the British were beaten, and had to recognize the independence of the colonies.

None could maintain that this compact paragraph was biased, yet the student reader emerges with no knowledge of the complexity of the issues that drove the colonists to revolt, of the arguments that could be advanced for and against the justice of their step, or of the idealism that motivated the men who drafted the Declaration of Independence and sacrificed so much for freedom. To misunderstand such a vital event in American history is to misunderstand America today as well as to misunderstand the dissolution of the British Empire in the twentieth century. Moreover it is to misunderstand what is at least of equal importance to historians: the impact of America on the mind of Europe in the eighteenth century.

While the paragraph cited is an extreme example, scarcely any discussion of the Revolution in an English textbook is sufficiently complete to make the American cause intelligible. Simply to list the events (which are after all the materials that form the basis for judgments without which an elementary survey is but a rope of sand) which are usually ignored is to reveal the inadequacy of the textbook discussions. Pontiac's Rebellion, the Proclamation Line of 1763, writs of assistance, Admiralty Courts, the Board of Customs Commissioners, the Sugar and Currency Acts, the Stamp Act Congress, the Townshend Duties, colonial protest against the Townshend Acts, the stationing of troops in Boston in 1768, the committees of correspondence, the *Gaspée* affair, the Intolerable Acts—all are omitted from at least one text and most from a majority of the books used today in the schools of England and Wales. So are the names of those principally concerned on both sides of the Atlantic; students read of George III and George Washington, but learn nothing of Grenville, Samuel Adams, and other architects of policy.

The military history of the Revolution fares only slightly better. A few of the more modern textbooks provide thumbnail sketches of the campaigns that make the outcome understandable, but far more mention only Lexington, Saratoga, and Yorktown. Some reduce the war to a few lines, as does the author who mentions Bunker Hill and Washington's retreat to Valley Forge, then sums up the remainder of the struggle in two brief paragraphs:

> The British, however, were at a disadvantage. They were 3,000 miles from home; they did not know this vast country; and their army was small. Their early successes came to an end with the surrender of a British force at Saratoga (1777) on the River Hudson. This was the moment chosen by France to join with the Americans against their old foes. The French

example was quickly followed by the Spanish and the Dutch, and Britain found her family affairs a centre of European interest.

The next disaster for Britain was loss of the command of the sea. It lasted for a moment, but that moment was fatal. Marching on Yorktown (1781), the British general found the French fleet lying outside—and not the British, as he had expected. On land he was surrounded by an American army. Surrender could not be avoided. 'It is all over! It is all over!' cried the British Prime Minister on hearing the news.

To hurry over eight years of history in this fashion is to distort the truth. To mention battles such as Saratoga without some detailed indication of their importance similarly violates the canons of scholarship. Surely a phrase explaining the impact of Burgoyne's defeat on France could be included, and would endow the account with some meaning. Simply to list the important battles omitted from the usual English textbooks— Trenton, Princeton, King's Mountain, the western campaigns —is to name most of the engagements of the war where American victories were won. Abbreviation may be necessary, but to carry it to the point of misrepresentation is propaganda twice compounded, not history by any standard.

(b) *Evidences of Anti-American Bias*

The authors of virtually all English textbooks obviously make every effort to free themselves from overt nationalistic bias, and on the whole succeed far better than their American counterparts. Now and then, however, nearly all succumb to an urge to glorify the British cause at the expense of the colonial, and a few vary from the general pattern in their almost open anti-American prejudices. It should be understood that evidence on this score is drawn from a small minority of those examined; they are certainly not representative of text-book writing in England and Wales.

Authors sometimes grow careless in the use of words, referring to the colonies as 'backward lands', an epithet hardly more suitable for 1760 than for 1960. One writer castigates the Bostonians who dumped the tea into the harbour as 'agitators', forgetting that such a word has modern connotations that did not apply at that time. Another speaks of the 'lawless defiance'

of the Americans when a less loaded phrase could easily have
been employed. Subconscious chauvinism permeates such remarks as one maintaining that Britian's 'professional army . . .
could be relied upon to beat the irregular levies of the rebels
whenever they fought on anything like equal terms'. To call
the rioters who touched off the Boston Massacre 'trouble
makers' is understandable, but one must remember that no
American patriot of the period would have used such a term.
Nor would the colonists have viewed the Declaration of
Independence as 'a propagandist appeal to liberals in every
country written with the particular hope of obtaining French
help in the war against Britain'. So it was, but such a one-sided
description ignores the idealism of its authors. Textbooks that
refer to British military victories as 'brilliant' or 'glorious'
similarly mirror the British viewpoint. Save in the older books,
these unfortunate phrases seem the result of traditionalism
rather than conscious prejudice.

The same might possibly be said of certain distortions or
omissions that seem designed to shed favourable light on the
British cause at the expense of the colonial. This can be said of
one author who describes the Boston Tea Party without
mentioning the Tea Act. Others twist the truth by suggesting
that unpopular minorities alone opposed English measures.
One in describing the opposition to the Stamp Act declares
that 'American lawyers, especially those of doubtful qualifica-
tions, were very prominent in stirring up bitter feeling against
the mother country', and goes on to add that the mob responsible for the Boston Massacre was composed entirely of sailors
who were 'ex-smugglers'. The parading of such distortions
without a single shred of evidence suggests that some English
authors were not above inventing facts to suit their prejudices.

Others pervert historical truth by less flagrant devices. One,
for instance, suggests that all violence was on one side by
dwelling on the Boston Tea Party and ignoring the Boston
Massacre, then piles inaccuracy on inaccuracy by stating
positively that an American militiaman fired the first shot at
Lexington. More commonly writers omit details that might
detract from their image of British ministers as always just and
British soldiers as consistently invincible. They list only the
Boston Port Act of 1774 as sole punishment for the Tea Party;

they charge that 'no one could have made a genuine grievance of the Tea Act'; they fail to mention that the attack on Bunker Hill did not succeed until the colonists ran out of powder; they explain the evacuation of Boston as the result of a food shortage rather than the fortification of Dorchester Heights; they assert that the Declaration of Independence was the work of 'extremists' who changed a family quarrel into a war for independence; and they slur over military events so successfully that the reader scarcely realizes that Britain lost an engagement until the final one of the war.

These errors, many the fruit of inadequate information rather than deliberate distortion, are relatively few, but when English authors turn to explaining their nation's defeat their latent national bias plays a more familiar role. For writers of any nation, let alone one with Britain's proud reputation, to admit that its armies were beaten by those of a third-rate power is to expect a miracle. So textbook authors grasp at straws to explain away the unpleasant truth: England lost because 'the armies were made up largely of hired German troops', or command of the sea was momentarily lost to the French while the land forces were doing well, or because the British fleet failed to arrive in time to pick up Cornwallis' army (with no mention of the reasons for the delay), or because British officers were trained in European tactics which failed in backwoods America (where actually nearly all battles followed European rules).

Authors apply this same technique to their descriptions of individual battles; an astounding variety of excuses are paraded to explain away each defeat. Lexington and Bunker Hill were only 'minor skirmishes'; the English withdrew from Philadelphia in 1778 because Burgoyne's campaign had taught them the need for caution; Burgoyne lost because the 'loyalists' deserted (apparently a reference to the Canadian troops). Some writers suggest that the British did not lose the Revolutionary war at all. One stresses Rodney's victory over De Grasse at the Battle of the Saints to argue that Britain's prestige had been fully restored at the close of hostilities. Another maintains that skilled British diplomats manipulated a peace that allowed the nation to retain 'most of her gains made in the mid-century wars'. These are rosy rationalizations, but they hardly mirror an international viewpoint, or indeed all the facts.

These examples of bias, it should be stressed, are gleaned from scores of textbooks used at all levels of secondary instruction in England and Wales. That they are fewer in number, and less blustering in tone, than those marring many American textbooks is obvious. The cases in which a British author consciously or unconsciously seeks to glorify his own country at the expense of others can be counted on the fingers of one hand, and are confined largely to older books badly in need of revision.

(c) *Bias in Reverse*

Some English authors, indeed, have leaned so far in the direction of fairness that they have distorted the picture in America's favour. Superpatriotic organizations in the United States would probably raise a mammoth hue and cry if a textbook illustrated its chapter on the Revolution with a flattering portrait of George III; yet one English book glorifies George Washington in this fashion. Others make the American general the hero of the war. He is praised as a 'heroic leader', 'an ideal leader', and 'a genius'. 'It is not often,' rhapsodizes one author, 'that a man can be said to have been so important in the history of his country that without him the whole of its future would have been different. In Great Britain this has been said of King Alfred, who saved the country from the Danes, and of King Henry VIII, who made it possible for the Protestant religion to replace the Catholic. Today one hundred and thirty million Americans rightly think of George Washington as the father of their nation. Without him, the colonies might indeed have become independent, but certainly not so soon. More important still, for them, they might never have become the *United* States of America.' One can appreciate the British reader who, after completing that passage, observed: 'This is a nice example of consolation in defeat: not only were we beaten by chaps who were really English, but also by an extraordinarily decent chap as American commander.' Bias in reverse can do as much harm as good.

This tone of pro-Americanism leads many of the English authors into outright errors, or at best half truths, favourable to

BRITISH SOLDIERS FORCING ENTRY

6. A modern drawing used in an American High School textbook suggests that the homes of the colonists were unsafe from British regulars.

7. In the original of this fine Copley portrait, Samuel Adams is pointing to the Massachusetts charter. The authors of an American High School textbook have distorted the truth in saying that he is 'pointing distainfully at some new evidence of British despotism'. (*Courtesy, City of Boston, deposited at Museum of Fine Arts, Boston.*)

8. A portrait of George Washington from p. 134 of Donald Lindsay and E. S. Washington, *A Portrait of Britain 1688-1851* (Clarendon Press, Oxford, 1954).

★ In 1814, the British General Ross entered Washington and "with that barbarism which distinguishes the Vandals of the middle ages, but which is unknown to civilized warfare, his troops burnt, not only the Capitol, which was in an unfinished state, but its extensive library and records appertaining not to war, but to peace and civilization." The quotation is from Willard's "History of the United States," published in 1842.

9. Inflammatory drawing used in a High School textbook in the United States, with a contemporary quotation accusing the British of 'barbarism which distinguishes the Vandals of the middle ages'.

the patriot cause. The colonies after 1763 were so absolutely governed that they had 'little to say in their own most important affairs'; the Townshend Acts were 'foolish'; the Hat Act 'prohibited' the manufacture of hats in the colonies; the British government tried to force the colonists to pay half the costs of the Seven Years' War; the British armies burned Philadelphia; the whole people of Boston were punished for the Tea Party, not simply the participants; the Navigation Acts banned all colonial trade with Europe and forced the colonists to ship only on British vessels; the Quebec Act was one of the Coercive Acts. These, and statements like them, would be branded as flagrantly nationalistic if they appeared in an American textbook.

Not content with glorifying George Washington and twisting facts to prove the rightness of his cause, a few English authors degrade George III to make him a proper villain. Witness this paragraph:

> But when George III became king (in 1760), he determined to alter all this [friendly relations between colonies and mother country]. He was going to be a despot, benevolent but firm, in America as in England. He decided that the colonies were to obey the Navigation Acts strictly. He even went further and tried to tax the Americans to pay for part of the cost of the Seven Years' War.

Should British youth be given such a distorted picture of one of their monarchs, and one so alien to the findings of modern scholarship? Should they be taught that George was determined to be a 'despot', when this was certainly not the case? Should they be told that the colonists were to be taxed to pay for the Seven Years' War when this was not the intention of the ministers? Writers may overflow with sympathy for the Americans, but they do a disservice to international understanding no less than to historical accuracy by such obvious distortions.

British textbook writers, despite their misplaced efforts in the direction of anti-nationalism, have by no means produced model accounts of the Revolution. Try though they do to avoid bias, they lean inevitably in one direction or the other. Even more serious is the distortion resulting from the brevity of their accounts and their deficient and often antiquated information. Surely the birth of a nation that was to influence Britain's future history so significantly deserves more than a few paragraphs in Britain's textbooks. The bare facts are there, but rarely is the young reader made aware of the motives or ideals of the revolutionists. Through omission and over-simplification the authors have committed sins that indict their books as sadly inadequate to meet the educational needs of today's shrinking world.

IV

THE WAR OF 1812

THE War of 1812 poses problems to textbook writers quite unlike those encountered in discussions of the American Revolution. Once more the Americans were the aggressors, declaring war after England (belatedly in view of the poor communications of the day) had made a final peaceful gesture by withdrawing decrees hostile to the interests of the United States. This time, however, the British triumphed; the Americans went to war to achieve certain ends that were not attained in the peace settlement. Once more the United States was divided, with ill-feeling between Federalists and Jeffersonians matching that between Loyalists and Patriots in the earlier conflict. Once more the military story is indecisive, with a succession of defeats and victories for both sides. And, to continue the comparison, each of these wars found Britain battling a whole concourse of enemies, and unable to concentrate her strength against her American foes.

Despite these similarities, textbook treatment of the Revolution and the War of 1812, as one might expect, differs greatly. In both England and America the Revolution was a major event. In the case of England it marked the end of the first British empire, turned the mother country to other areas, modified the outlook on the portions of the western empire still retained (the West Indies and Canada), and influenced economic and imperial attitudes and policies for generations. For America the all-important consequence of the Revolution was independence. Hence students in both nations would expect, and receive, a fairly heavy dosage of Revolutionary history— less indeed than is warranted in British books, but still enough for study in some depth. The War of 1812 presents a striking contrast. In American textbooks as in American history it is a major event, marking a turning point in the nation's history and kindling the nationalistic spirit that governed for a century beyond. 'The Star Spangled Banner' was only one manifestation of the nationalism that flamed during and after the war. For Britain the War of 1812 was a minor irritant, notable primarily for the bad faith of the Americans in declaring war when Great Brtain was locked in a death struggle with Napoleon. British writers therefore pay scant attention to this insignificant diversion, contenting themselves with brief mention in contrast to the much longer, often chapter-length discussions in American books.

Against this background, we can turn to the evidences of nationalistic bias detected in the textbooks of the two nations as their authors describe the War of 1812. This will reveal that American writers can be inspired to patriotic fervour by a minor as by a major war, and that bias by omission or commission is to be found in most of their accounts. And it will show that English authors, by paying too scant attention to the War of 1812, have failed to provide their readers with a meaningful story of a conflict that was to influence the world of the future, including Great Britain itself and its imperial world.

I. AMERICAN JUNIOR HIGH SCHOOL TEXTBOOKS

Accounts of the War of 1812 vary in length in Junior High school texts from four to eight pages, an allotment of space insufficient to allow ample treatment of the war in America's overall history. As a result they are usually superficial, and guilty of omitting such essential items as the economic policies of the United States that influenced the outbreak of the struggle, the complexity of forces creating a war spirit, the American losses on the battlefields, the sectional feelings engendered, and the significance of the peace. Instead most authors seem content to stress British impressment of seamen as the sole cause of the war, to glorify a few American heroes and victories, and to dwell overlong on Francis Scott Key and the writing of the 'Star Spangled Banner'. This may be useful propaganda, but it is not good history.

Historians today recognize that the War of 1812 was the result of a complex of forces both internal and external: British and French interference with neutral trade, impressment, a desire for Canada as a pawn to force Britain to relax her trade restrictions, and the insistence of the West that only war would end Indian attacks. To simplify the story by naming only one of these causes, and then often erroneously or inadequately, as most Junior High school textbooks do, is to warp the truth. One text states categorically that the United States went to war to seize Canada; this was necessary, it goes on, because British agents were stirring the red men to attack frontier outposts. Such an oversimplification is as inaccurate as it is biased. It unjustly blames England for inciting the Indians, when actually a series of land-grabbing treaties (not mentioned in the text) goaded them into war; it ignores the maritime factors that alone explain the degree of war fever in the United States and the sectional divisions within the nation; it hides the disgraceful conduct of the New England Federalists even to the point of omitting all mention of the Hartford Convention. The result is to create a pro-American, anti-British attitude that the facts do not warrant.

Discussions in other textbooks are not much better. Impressment, rather than Indian attacks, is usually singled out as the basic cause of America's just anger, with English attacks on shipping in a secondary rôle. This is all very well, for these British policies did arouse the resentment that fed the war spirit in the United Sates. But competent historians today would temper this one-sided account with other essential items of information. They would not assert that 'American rights' were violated by England's maritime decrees for to do so would be to display an ignorance of international law as understood at the time. They would show that between 1806 and 1812 France seized more American ships than did England. They would point out that the desertion rate was so high on British vessels in American ports that the nation's salvation depended on holding or recovering its sailors. They would reveal that the vast majority of those impressed were British deserters, not Americans as one textbook implies and another states. These are well-known facts that deserve mention in any impartial history.

An impartial treatment would also enlighten its readers on the world situation, telling something of the titanic struggle between France and Britain. It would tell them of the determination of each antagonist to starve the other into submission by any means necessary, for niceties of international law have been ignored in every major war in history where national survival was at stake. It would make them aware of the Berlin and Milan decrees of France as well as the Orders in Council of England, and of the efforts of the United States to bring both powers to terms by the use of the embargo and other devices. Knowledge of these policies is essential for an understanding of both sectionalism within the United States and Napoleon's trickery through the Cadore Letter. Just as important, it would reveal that England repealed its Orders in Council two days before the declaration of war, a backdown rare in the annals of warfare and indicative of that country's desire for peace. Stress on these simple facts, lacking in every Junior High school textbook, would go far to alter the traditional picture of an aggressive Britain trampling on American 'rights'.

A similar nationalistic bias mars the descriptions of the military events of the War of 1812. Admittedly, space limitations preclude detailed treatment of the several campaigns. In selecting those to be included, however, impartiality demands two things: the story of the burning of parts of Washington by the British (which is always emphasized, usually as a backdrop for an account of Francis Scott Key and the 'Star Spangled Banner') should be countered by a discussion of the earlier burning of York, Canada, by the Americans; and the few spectacular naval victories earned by American vessels should be balanced by the story of the British triumphs that eventually drove the United States ships from the seas. Without the inclusion of these facts, the outcome of the war is not understandable. American readers, fed on a diet of American triumphs, and conversely British readers aware only of their own successes, might well wonder how such an indecisive peace was possible.

Nearly all Junior High school textbooks fail to provide this balance. All describe at some length the burning of the government buildings at Washington, but only one emphasizes the fact that the British attack was in retaliation for the destruction of York. Naval battles are treated in the same one-sided fashion. The exploits of the *Constitution* against the *Guerrière*, and the 'smashing' (in the word of one author) victory of Oliver Hazard Perry on Lake Erie are never omitted, but only one book mentions the defeat of the *Chesapeake* by the *Shannon*, and then apparently only as an excuse to repeat the command of the American captain: 'Don't give up the ship.' Reluctant admission is made that the United States navy was swept from the seas, but usually with the added comment that the sheer weight of the British force alone made this possible. To say, as does one author, that American victories 'raised questions about the fighting ability of the British navy' is to draw a conclusion not warranted by the facts.

These weighted accounts of naval engagements typify the treatment of military events in every textbook. Most assume a garb of impartiality when they mention British victories in Canada and the East, but the general effect is of history deliberately or subconsciously distorted to favour the United States. True, no textbook at this level can tell the whole complex story of military and naval engagements. But to single out *only* those battles that lend themselves to patriotic prose—the triumph of the *Constitution* over the *Guerrière*, Perry's victory on Lake Erie, the Battle of the Thames, Andrew Jackson's victory at New Orleans—is to distort the truth. All err in this direction, although fortunately few go so far as one author who allots to the Battle of Lake Erie one-quarter of the space devoted to the entire war. The American military record in the War of 1812 was no better than it should have been, and justice demands that British troops—no less than the incompetence, unpreparedness, and division of the American people—should be given credit for this.

Few textbooks at the Junior High school level do more than mention the peace, and none openly admits that the United States suffered a technical defeat by failing to achieve the objectives for which it declared war. Attention is paid to the agreements between England and the United States that followed the Treaty of Ghent, and proper credit is allotted them as models of international understanding. But the broader impact of the struggle on the American psychology—so important to an understanding of subsequent events—fails to find a place in any textbook. So also does the fact that this was a second War for Independence which won for the United States economic freedoms as important as the political freedoms achieved in 1783. These are essential interpretations that deserve a place in any textbook.

2. AMERICAN HIGH SCHOOL TEXTBOOKS

Nearly all texts used in American high schools devote a full chapter to the War of 1812. The result is a more balanced treatment than those found in books designed for Junior High school use, with proper attention paid to the causes of the war, the military victories on both sides, and the significance of the peace. The relative lack of bias in these volumes provides striking proof of the fact that nationalistic distortions are partly the result of over-condensation and that an author with space to tell both sides of the story is usually willing to do so. This does not, however, free the High school texts of all guilt. In numerous instances authors reveal lack of knowledge of recent interpretations, particularly in discussing the origins of the war. More are guilty of subconscious bias when describing military victories; the temptation to praise American successes as 'brilliant' without awarding the enemy similar accolades is too persuasive to be completely avoided. Many, too, fail to recognize the importance of the war in the emergence of an independent American foreign policy, which today's historians label its most significant long-term effect.

The failure of authors to mirror the latest findings on the causes of the War of 1812 is understandable, for few events in America's past have been so often re-interpreted. Historians over the past generation have ascribed the conflict to the violation of American neutral rights by England, impressment, the land hunger of frontiersmen, Indian wars in the West and a desire to wipe out the Canadian bases of their operations, an economic depression in the Ohio Valley, the failure of communications between Britain and the United States, and the hope that a conquered Canada could be used as a pawn to force England to relax her trade decrees. Today most scholars lean to the maritime interpretation as most logical, although recognizing that sentiment for war was bred by the depression, by land hunger, and especially by a desire to check Indian attacks.

Most of the High school textbooks fail to mirror this historical revisionism. Instead they stress, as did historians a generation ago, land hunger and the Indian problem as basic causes of the war. This interpretation ignores the fact that the western War Hawks were few in Congress, and that the votes for the declaration came from the mid-Atlantic and southern seaboard states. There lived the men who had voted for Jefferson's punitive measures since 1806, but by 1812 realized that economic sanctions were insufficient. The nation's honour could be defended, they saw, and the nation saved from relapse to colonial trade status, only by refusing to yield to the maritime policies of the warring powers. War would allow the conquest of Canada, which would have the dual results of ending Indian attacks on the Northwest and providing the United States with a tool to force England's hand. That province would be returned when the British ministers agreed to respect American neutral rights on the high seas.

This modern explanation of American attitudes answers many questions left unanswered by earlier interpretations. Yet it is used in not a single textbook. Instead the most popular explanation of the war spirit is the desire of Americans for Canada to quell Indian raids. Some textbooks explain war sentiment in the South by assuming that Southerners wanted Florida to stop Indian attacks from there; historians today agree that these raids were so few that they did not engender such a demand. Most authors are both sufficiently informed and impartial to point out that the Indian attackers who used Canada as their headquarters were neither armed nor incited by British agents, although a few imply the oppposite and one gratuitously suggests that 'rightly or wrongly, many Westerners believed that British officials in Canada were backing Tecumseh's confederacy'. To say that Westerners believed a thing is one thing; to suggest that they might have been right when all scholarship proves them wrong is another.

Similar examples of bias by innuendo mar textbook accounts of the Indian warfare that preceded general hostilities. For an author to state that British guns found on warriors killed at the Battle of Tippecanoe convinced Americans that 'the Englishmen were up to their old tricks: plotting with the Indians against the frontiersmen', or for another to write that these

guns proved to frontiersmen that 'the British were inciting the
Indians to war on settlers in the Northwest' is to stoop to a most
unfortunate form of misrepresentation. Equally misleading is
the remark that William Henry Harrison's victory strengthened
western belief that the English 'had been inciting the Indians
. . . ever since St. Clair's defeat twenty years before'. To hide
behind such phrases as 'Westerners believed', without pointing
out the falsity of such beliefs, is to obscure the truth. Common
sense, as well as ample documentation, proves that Great
Britain would never have courted war with the United States
by goading the Indians into attacks on the settlements just
when it was locked in a death struggle with Napoleon. The
Indians did fall on the frontier outposts, but only because their
lands were being stripped from them by fraudulent treaties.
This essential bit of information is missing from a vast majority
of the textbooks.

Authors seem equally incapable of presenting the impressment issue impartially. To do so, they must of necessity emphasize two things. One is the plight in which Great Britain found
itself; with her very existence dependent on her ability to
maintain sea lanes, she would be committing national suicide
if she did not take vigorous action to check the desertions in
American ports that weakened her naval strength. Under these
life-or-death circumstances, her reliance on the doctrine of
'indelible allegiance' to press into service deserters who had
become American citizens is understandable, especially since
forged citizenship papers were readily purchasable in the
United States and were even offered to British sailors as an
inducement to desert. The other is that France could not
impress American seamen because of the language difference.
That nation's interference with neutral trade suggests that she
would have been just as willing to swell the ranks of her ships'
crews as England if able to do so. Impartiality also demands
that the often-quoted figure of 6,000 impressments (borrowed
from James Madison who was hardly an objective witness) be
balanced by statistics on the number of desertions from the
British navy. Current scholarship concludes that more deserted
than were pressed into service; it would also quarrel with a
textbook author who says that only ten per cent of those impressed were British subjects, let alone the writer who asserts

that the figure should be increased to one in every ten thousand.

Britain's interference with American vessels carrying supplies to France or French possessions is mentioned by most textbooks as a factor inviting war, and rightly so. Objectivity demands, however, that the story of these confiscations be tempered by information which, while not exonerating England, at least accounts for her actions. The student should be made aware that French privateers were as eager to prey on United States merchantmen as English men of war and somewhat more successful in doing so. France seized more American ships during the embargo than Great Britain. This essential fact is ignored by every textbook writer. Fairness also dictates that England's precedents for her Orders in Council be mentioned, including the Rule of 1756; to say as one author does that these decrees were invented solely to curb American trade is to be unmindful of past events. Finally, and most important, textbook accounts of the neutrality controversy should underline the fact that the United States insisted on trading with Britain's enemy at a time when that nation's survival depended on choking off such commerce. Actions of any country in such an emergency cannot be those expected in normal times; today's philosophy of national survival by any means is deeply rooted in the past. Thus an author who states that the United States 'had no alternative but submission or war' would be more accurate if he had added another alternative: that Americans cease trading with England's enemy.

Some lack of understanding persists as textbook authors detail the final events leading to war. Nearly all mention Napoleon's Cadore letter, a device that allows them to observe quite properly that pressure from the War Hawks was not the sole force leading to Madison's declaration of war. Several deplore the conflict, calling it an 'unnecessary' struggle or branding the declaration 'an act of dubious wisdom'. Yet these same authors state that a better communications system, allowing the United States to learn that the Orders in Council had been revoked, would have allowed a peaceable settlement of differences; some who follow this line of reasoning apparently forget that they have accepted the expansionist interpretation as a cause of the conflict. In dealing with the final diplomatic phases, authors usually ignore the Erskine Agreement which marked the parting of the ways, and fail to mention Francis James Jackson whose conduct helped to widen the breach between Britain and the United States.

The military history of the War of 1812 is usually compressed into two or three pages that are unmarred by the excessive patriotism that marks the parallel sections in Junior High school textbooks. Nearly all try to paint an objective picture, and most dwell on American defeats as well as American victories. Yet there are unfortunate deviations from this rule; one volume describes four naval victories by the United States without mentioning a single defeat, and another lists five American triumphs while arguing that the one defeat mentioned—the *Chesapeake*'s fight with the *Shannon*—was really a draw. There is a tendency in a few books to glorify the few American naval victories by stressing the vast strength of Great Britain; one places English superiority at the ratio of 2,000 to 16, another at 20 to 1, and a third at 800 to 12. All this ignores the fact that most of Britain's fighting ships were engaged in waters near the Continent, and that the difference in strength in American waters was minimal. The defeat of the *Guerrière* by the *Chesapeake* is sometimes allotted greater space and more impassioned adjectives than the English victories that drove the American navy from the seas.

Land engagements are also sometimes coloured by the subconscious national bias of the author. Isaac Brock, the capable Canadian commander, is seldom mentioned, but pages are lavished on William Henry Harrison, Oliver Hazard Perry, and Andrew Jackson. Every textbook describes the burning of Washington's public buildings, but at least three fail to mention the prior burning of York, and one that does so wrongly names the city and omits the fact that it was the capital of Upper Canada. Jackson's victory at New Orleans is pictured as 'brilliant' and 'the most important of the war and one of the most brilliant victories in our history'; it also 'demonstrated that American soldiers were a match for the best British troops'. Strategists might agree on Andrew Jackson's skills as a commander, but they would point out that several British generals won engagements where they displayed just as much tactical knowledge—without earning acclaim from American textbook writers. Nor do authors mention one vital factor: that Britain's principal armies, officers, and attention were concentrated on the Continent. Only one makes the mistake of saying that after October, 1813, the British were free to direct their entire energies against the United States.

In describing the War of 1812, American textbook writers have made an honest effort to avoid national bias, and to paint a reasonably accurate picture of what occurred. They have failed for two reasons. Most are unfamiliar with the latest historical studies on the conflict, which tend to place Britain in a better light. And most are unable to divorce themselves from the national value scales which transform American successes into 'brilliant victories' or trigger memory failures when the time comes to describe enemy triumphs. These authors, no less than those castigating George III or lauding the Founding Fathers, are unable to sever themselves from the traditions in which they have been reared. Until they learn to view events on both sides of the Atlantic without prejudice, the history that they write will be tainted by nationalistic bias.

3. BRITISH SECONDARY SCHOOL TEXTBOOKS

Textbook writers in England and Wales can scarcely be expected to devote extensive space to such a minor event in Britain's long history as the War of 1812, yet their indifference to that conflict and the historical distortions that result prove them guilty of 'bias by omission' to an alarming degree. That war is not even mentioned in several texts; in the remainder it is described in passages varying from a sentence to a page or two. To say of this conflict *only* that Wellington was handicapped because 'the best of his veterans had been sent to fight in a war which had broken out between Britain and the United States of America', or that 'this led to a short, ignominious war (1812–1814) between England and the United States, which as a neutral country objected to Britain's claim to board and search her ships', is to surrender to national bias as flagrant as that of the flag-waving superpatriot. A student reader is left with the impression that an event of major significance to one nation is so insignificant to another that it can be shrugged away with a condescending phrase. Another writer who dismisses the war as 'the American scuffle' is equally guilty of half-way vision.

Passing references such as these conceal from the British student the fact that to the Americans the War of 1812 was an event of major importance and of significance to Great Britain and its empire as well. Within the United States it initiated a revolution in national psychology that started the nation along the road to its future status as a world power, as well as solidifying a foreign policy that was to endure for a century. Its impact on Canada was almost as great, spurring internal developments, engendering new attitudes towards the empire, and ushering in an era of peace in Canadian-American relations. To Great Britain the war meant new soul-searching in the reappraisal of empire relationships. And in any case, the War of 1812 was the outcome of a great commercial and maritime struggle against Napoleon, and should not be omitted from the larger history of that conflict. A fuller discussion of the struggle in British textbooks is long overdue.

Before these accounts can be written, authors in England and Wales must learn far more about the War of 1812 than they know today. Even the fuller treatments of the conflict in texts are both woefully inadequate and sprinkled with errors of fact and interpretation that render them unsatisfactory. Typical is the following:

> The causes of this war were threefold: a general hatred of the English, kept alive by one party in the States ever since the War of Independence; our insistence on searching American ships for escaped English seamen; and the Orders in Council, which practically cut off the Americans from trade with France. It is typical of the general futility of this war that the Orders in Council were dropped when the Russian campaign seemed likely to end the Continental System—just too late to prevent the outbreak of hostilities between England and America. These hostilities, however, did not amount to very much. The United States showed themselves to be a seafaring nation by winning a number of small naval engagements and capturing many of our merchant-ships, though the once-famous contest of the *Shannon* and the *Chesapeake* was a victory for the British. But when the Americans invaded Canada in great force, the Canadian militia and some British regulars combined to drive them out. In the later stages of the war a British army landed

and deliberately burnt the public buildings of Washington, for which the Americans had their revenge at New Orleans, where a large body of veteran troops from the Peninsula was cut to pieces before strong entrenchments. In fact, the main significance of the American War of 1812 is that it seemed to most English people to be a cowardly attack upon us when we were already fighting against great odds.

Such truncated accounts as this—and many others like it in the textbooks of England and Wales—reveal the danger of over-compact writing. Inevitably they exhibit bias in favour of the home country which, with a little more space and much more care, could be avoided.

This is shown in both the accounts written by English authors of the causes of the War of 1812 and the military events. Text-book writers seem completely unaware of the reasons why the United States declared war; resentment against British policies on the high seas is generally mentioned, but the complexity and multiplicity of issues is not even suggested. To ascribe America's declaration of war to 'resentment of her exclusion from European trade', or to indignation over impressment is to reveal only a small fraction of the truth. No English schoolboy could understand the attitude of the United States without knowing that the frontiersmen believed the British guilty of stirring Indian attacks upon them, but not a single volume mentions this fact. Completely ignored, too, is the land hunger of the Westerners, and the hope that a conquered Canada could serve as a pawn to win respect for the rights of neutral shippers. To brand the war as 'unnecessary' as many British authors do is to ignore the whole psychology of the American people at the time.

Bias of the same sort distorts discussions of the military events of the war, again because space limitations preclude any adequate descriptions. The few that mention any naval engagements by name describe the victory of the *Shannon* over the *Chesapeake*, omitting any reference to the *Constitution*'s triumph over the *Guerrière*. Land campaigns are mishandled just as badly; one of the few textbooks to deal with military events makes much of the failure of the three American attempts to invade Canada but fails to mention the American victory at the Thames. The assault on Washington receives proper attention, but several authors minimize the attack by saying that only the capitol was burned; actually the White House and several other government buildings were put to the torch. Only two currently used textbooks deem the Battle of New Orleans worthy of description, and one adds that its principal importance was to make Andrew Jackson look to the Americans 'like a great military hero'. Not a single book pays sufficient attention to the peace treaty, or even hints at the effect of the war on American foreign policy or the internal growth of the nation.

These accounts of the War of 1812 in British textbooks tellingly illustrate the dangers of over-condensation. Admittedly, this was a minor war in Britain's long history, and an annoying one as well. Admittedly, too, textbooks dealing with the history of any one country cannot be expected to explore the histories of every nation with which that country enjoys contact; such a practice would convert every national history into world history. But brevity does tempt subconscious exhibitions of nationalistic bias, for if an author has space to mention only one battle he will instinctively select one that his heroes have won. Until the textbooks of England and Wales recognize that the War of 1812 played a part in world history by starting the United States along the road to its present place as a world power, and that events of such subsequent importance must be described if the citizen of today's world is to understand the many nations that decide his fate, they will contribute to the distortions that hamper cordial understanding in Anglo-American relationships.

During the War of 1812, British troops burned and plundered Havre de Grace (above) before marching on Washington and burning the Capitol. The naval battle between the U.S.S. *Constitution* and the British *Guerrière* (right) was one of the single-ship engagements which demonstrated the fighting ability of the American frigates and their superior gunnery. At Fort McHenry, after a terrific bombardment (below), in the 'rockets' red glare, . . . the flag was still there," and the British invaders retired.

10. One page from a leading American High School textbook, showing the British about to burn Washington, the victory of the *Constitution* over the *Guerrière*, and the scene that inspired the 'Star-Spangled Banner'—an arrangement obviously designed to stimulate patriotism rather than understanding.

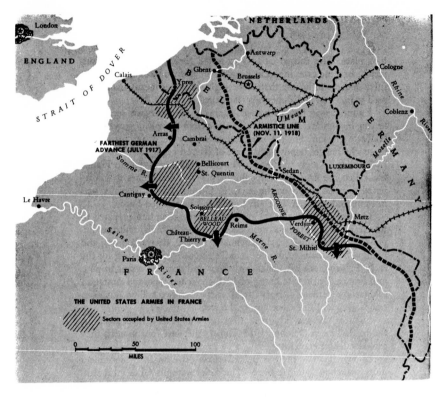

On this map of Europe during World War I name the areas occupied by the United States armies. Through which sector did the Armistice Line pass?

11. Map of the World War I battlefields used in a Junior High School textbook, with no indication that armies of the other Allies were even present.

V

THE FIRST WORLD WAR
1914-1918

THE First World War presents a quite different challenge to textbook writers on both sides of the Atlantic than that presented by the American Revolution or the War of 1812. During the Revolution and the 1812 war Great Britain and the United States were enemies; in describing these conflicts innate prejudices nudge English and American authors alike into accounts that glorify their own land at the expense of the other. In the First World War, on the other hand, Britain and the United States fought side by side against the Central Powers, at least during the few months between active American participation and the armistice. Latent British prejudices against the people and government of the United States, and traditional American suspicion of the English, would play a small part in this situation.

Yet the manner in which textbook writers describe the First World War is almost as dangerous to Anglo-American understanding as the biased treatments accorded to the Revolution and the War of 1812. It is true that the secondary school books used in the United States are *relatively* lucid, impartial, and free of anti-British sentiments when contrasted with their prejudiced descriptions of the earlier conflicts. But British textbooks present a different picture, for hostility to the United States is apparent in some and only partly concealed in others. Moreover, in scarcely any book is there complete freedom from bias of one sort or another.

This exhibits itself in two rather obvious ways. First, American authors and British authors alike tend to write in a nationalistic vacuum, manifesting concern only for events transpiring within their own countries or directly involving their own people, and indifferent to (or perhaps even unaware of) happenings beyond. American writers show little concern for placing the war in its proper historical setting, or revealing the part played by Great Britain in the complex of alliances that exploded in 1914. Some are so little interested in the events in Europe that preceded American entry in 1917 that a reader might suppose the war to have begun in that year. Second, authors in both nations tend to emphasize the contribution to victory made by their own countries, and to minimize that of the other. A few of the more unbalanced American books give the impression that the American expeditionary force began fighting a year before it did, turned the tide of victory, and suffered casualties out of all proportion to their numbers. A few English textbooks leave the reader with the feeling that the war would have been won without American aid, which is hardly mentioned. Even though excessive distortions are in the minority, all textbooks, however unwittingly, reveal traces of the desire to monopolize glory for the author's homeland.

I. AMERICAN JUNIOR HIGH SCHOOL TEXTBOOKS

In the most widely used Junior High school texts, accounts of the First World War vary in length from four or five pages to twenty or more, with the majority favouring the shorter treatment. A few submerge their descriptions of the war into other and scarcely relevant topics. One such volume devotes three-quarters of a chapter to the growth of democracy in Europe during the nineteenth and twentieth centuries, immigration to the United States, and the outbreak of the war in Europe; the remaining quarter deals with British and German raids on American shipping, the sinking of the *Lusitania*, the events of January, 1917, the declaration of war three months later, and American aid to the allies which began (says this misguided author) after the United States had entered the conflict. Other textbooks are more orthodox chronologically, but no more thorough in their coverage.

Most of this sort adopt an episodic rather than a narrative technique, a device that allows authors to dwell overlong on items that interest them, and to omit others that may be of far greater interest or importance. One reprints an entire short story by Alfred Noyes on submarine warfare which, while doubtless enlightening and probably capable of producing elevated thoughts in the young, occupies a deal of space that might better have been used to tell the reader something about the war. Others hurry over military events so rapidly that the resulting chronicle is meaningless; the result is to give an impression of a series of American victories with a few slight assists from the Allies. One author credits the United States with winning two of the six 'drives' in which they engaged, and of contributing significantly to the others. In some textbooks no mention is made of the peace efforts of Woodrow Wilson, or of the President's heroic efforts to create an international organization. Nearly all would be improved with a more analytical appraisal of the forces that led the United States into the war, and with some discussion of life on the home front.

In addition to these shortcomings, three evidences of national bias appear with alarming frequency. Nearly all texts imply that the American army became effective in Europe far sooner than it did, thus denying the Allies credit for holding back the Central Powers until May 28, 1918 when massive American forces first became active. March, 1918, is a favoured date with most authors who write that the expeditionary force assumed the brunt of fighting from that time on, although one places Americans in the front line trenches as early as October, 1917, without mentioning that this was a token force. Secondly, no textbook gives evidence on the casualties among *all* the Allies; to present statistics on American dead and wounded alone obscures the fact that England, France, and other nations sacrificed far more than the United States. A simple table would supply this information, and would be more effective than some of the many cartoons that crowd information from the pages of present volumes; similar tables on the comparative economic losses of the warring nations would also reveal the contributions of each nation. Thirdly, no textbook pays proper attention to the burdens carried by Britain and France for the three years before the United States entered the war; many create the impression that the conflict began with the arrival of American troops.

While the peace efforts of all the major powers are properly recognized in most texts, one does state that all the Big Four leaders save Woodrow Wilson 'were more eager to get advantages for their own countries than to help make a better world' —a statement impossible to prove even if true. Several hint that the selfish territorial demands of the Allies contrasted with the selfless idealism of the United States at the peace table, but this point is not stressed.

On the whole, the First World War is treated by the authors of Junior High school textbooks with greater impartiality than they are able to muster in describing the Revolution or the War of 1812. On the whole they stand acquitted of any serious nationalistic bias in discussing Anglo-American relations, although all are guilty of some 'bias by omission' and all would benefit by more extended treatments, more exact knowledge of events, and the inclusion of comparative statistics on casualties and expenditures of the Allies.

2. AMERICAN HIGH SCHOOL TEXTBOOKS

American participation in the First World War is generally allotted a full chapter in textbooks used in High schools in the United States. This space allotment allows a more balanced treatment than is common at the lower educational levels, with proper attention paid to the forces that led to American participation, adequate discussion of miliary events and of affairs on the home front, and sufficient analysis of the peace negotiations to make them understandable. Most texts are relatively free of nationalistic bias, although many have little favourable to say of Germany. The contrast between a single author's chapters on the American Revolution and the First World War is sometimes startling; the British blunderers and oppressors of one era have become the saviours and splendid companions of another. Yet minor evidences of bias do appear, and deserve mention.

One or two textbooks fail to explain the creation and functioning of the pre-war alliances, thus creating the impression that Britain was fully committed to a partnership with France and Russia when this was not the case. Nor was Great Britain a part of Europe's armed camp, and fully prepared for war, as suggested by several authors. Proper treatment of this period would require a fairly complete explanation of the workings of the Triple Entente, and of Britain's rôle in the diplomacy of the 1890–1914 era, as well as of the alliances and events that led directly to war. It would also reveal the peace efforts in Europe and the United States during those years, a subject adequately discussed in only one text. Certainly to dismiss the whole peace effort with the cynical remark that 'After the close of the nineteenth century, Europeans talked loudly about international peace while they busily prepared for a world war which they really did not believe they could avoid' is to distort history and obstruct internationalism.

Most authors make a conscientious attempt to paint an objective picture of Britain's interference with American shipping in the years after 1914, balancing this properly against the German submarine attacks. One author, thus, although stating that British 'abuses of our rights as a neutral . . . came close to rupturing relations,' acknowledges that they could not give up their principal weapon, and that the practice of taking vessels into port for examination was 'reasonable' under the new conditions of submarine warfare. The distinction is also drawn between property losses and the loss of lives caused by German U-Boats. Carping critics might wish that some authors had clarified their discussion of 'contraband', and described the types of goods placed on 'the list' by Great Britain, but perhaps not too much detail can be given in High school textbooks.

More serious is the failure of several authors to point out the long delay between American entry into the war and active troop participation in the conflict. True, a few units of the First Division were ready for combat by October 21, 1917, but not until May 28, 1918, did the massive use of American forces against the Central Powers begin. This is clearly stated in only two textbooks; the remainder either assign an incorrect date early in 1918 or blur the whole point by such vague statements as 'The fresh American troops often played a vital part in extensive engagements during the late fall of 1917', or 'Soon after our entry into the war, a citizen army of Americans was prepared and moved to French battlefields'. The thirteen months that elapsed between these two events can hardly be termed 'soon'. Another author creates a similarly false impression when he reports the arrival of a handful of American soldiers in Paris in June, 1917, and adds: 'Their appearance in the battle line unquestionably heartened the Allies and seriously shook the morale of the Germans'. Such statements deny those Allies proper credit for holding back the Central Powers during the grim winter of 1917–1918.

Like the Junior High school textbooks, many of those used in the High schools of the United States fail to report comparative statistics on the losses in men and money suffered by the Allied powers. Only three indicate in one way or another that those of France and Britain far surpassed those of the United States. Tables summarizing casualties and expenditures would bring home to the student the greater sacrifices made by the European Allies. Moreover, not a single textbook mentions the major contribution to the war effort made by the Dominions, despite the fact that Canada's involvement for the four long years of the war drained that country's resources proportionately far beyond the cost to the United States.

More damaging is the subconscious tendency of American textbook authors to employ weighted words while describing military events. One describes the 'overwhelming victory' won by the United States forces at St. Mihiel, then lamely adds that 'British and French forces met with equal success'. Another holds that American supplies given the Allies 'made the victory possible', and that American troops 'turned the tide of battle'. Still another believes that 'America's entry into the war proved to be the decisive factor in the war's outcome'. All of these statements express partial truth, but the impression left with the reader is that the United States won the war almost single-handed. The addition of a word or two—'American troops helped to make the victory possible'—would contribute to both truth and understanding. One author demonstrates the effectiveness of this technique when, after describing the contributions to victory made by the United States, he adds: 'Important though they were, the American victories represented only part of the tremendous offensive against the crumbling German lines. The Belgians, British, and French, confident now of victory, were fighting fiercely along the entire front'. The Allied victory was a joint effort, and should be so recognized.

Just as some authors imply that the United States was largely responsible for victory, so do a few paint Woodrow Wilson as the only crusader for a just peace. One textbook fails to mention any other member of the Big Four save Lloyd George, who is dismissed as 'brilliant but unstable'. Happily this is the exception, for most recognize that each Allied power was capably represented, and that realism rather than greed dictated their actions at the peace conference.

Like their counterparts at the Junior High school level, the High school textbooks deal far more objectively with the First World War than with the American Revolution or the War of 1812. The reason for this is painfully obvious: the story of the Revolution has been encrusted with myth and legend by generations of earlier historians and story-tellers until the kernels of truth are both hard to find and unpalatable to an audience bred from childhood on sturdier fare. The murderous wars of the twentieth century, on the other hand, do not lend themselves to heroic glorification. To strip away a veneer of untruth about earlier days is far more difficult than to tell the truth about a more recent event.

3. BRITISH SECONDARY SCHOOL TEXTBOOKS

Attitudes reflected by the textbook writers of England and Wales are exactly the opposite of their American counterparts; they succeed in describing the American Revolution with a measure of objectivity but abandon all pretence of impartiality when recounting the story of the First World War. Planting themselves squarely in England, they content themselves with tracing the major rôle that British armies and the British navy dlayed in saving the world from Teutonic despotism; they pay little attention to France and credit the United States with only a slight assistance. With one or two notable exceptions, no English textbook attempts to explain the American contributions to an Allied victory, or part in the peace settlement. Some fail even to mention that the United States entered the war. This is not only a distortion of history, but a flagrant example of the worst form of 'bias by omission'.

A proper discussion of the First World War in the textbooks of England and Wales should, of course, give adequate weight to the burdens borne by the nation's army, navy, and civilian population. But it should recognize that this burden was not carried alone; France, Belgium, Italy, Imperial Russia, the Dominions, and the United States should be assigned their proper shares of credit for the victory. A well-balanced text-book should include a discussion of the widespread American sympathy for the Allied cause and the weakening of those sentiments with Britain's interference with trade. It should explain the American loans and other aid granted Great Britain between 1914 and 1917, and make clear the nation's rôle as a neutral carrier for the Allies despite interference by the British navy. It should describe Woodrow Wilson's doctrine of 'strict accountability', and the part this played in swinging the country toward participation after unrestricted submarine warfare began. In dealing with military events, a well-planned text should relate the American contributions in fighting men and ships, the campaigns in which they participated with some indication of the relative numbers involved, and the idealistic rôle of Wilson as a peacemaker and architect of a League of Nations which might have created a better world than the one that emerged. To include all of this information in a brief account—and English textbooks vary from four or five pages to a brief chapter on the war as a whole—is to test the ingenuity of an author, but to omit it is to distort the truth so badly that overt bias would be mild by comparsison.

The bill of particulars that may be summoned against the textbooks of England and Wale is startlingly complete. Readers will search in vain for anything approaching a complete account of the contributions to an Allied victory made by the United States between 1914 and 1917; whether of sentiment, loans, or supplies, all of which played a part in bolstering British opposition to Germany. A majority of the books also fail to mention British interference with neutral shipping, or to deal with the whole complex controversy over neutral rights that plagued relations between the two countries. At the same time, however, German submarine warfare is properly given full attention. Such lack of balance persuades an uninformed reader that the United States delayed entry into the war because its isolationist tendencies made it unwilling to aid a sister democracy.

One example of this type of distortion will demonstrate the degree of national bias:

At the outbreak of war Americans, under their President Woodrow Wilson, were certain that European affairs were no concern of theirs. Since the days of Washington America had been determined not to become entangled in European politics. Wilson urged his countrymen to be not only neutral in action, but neutral in speech and thought. A former university professor, he gave the impression of regarding all European politics as beneath his notice and he sometimes spoke as though there was no great gulf separating the actions of Germany from those of Britain and France. The sufferings of Belgium appeared to him little different from those of Ireland.

To ascribe such sentiments to Wilson is to do historical accurac's a disservice. So is the author's disregard of the Presidenty policy of 'strict accountability', and his failure even to mention the effect on the United States of Britain's interference with neutral shipping. He adds insult to injustice when he counters his account of the entry of the United States into the war with a snide comment: 'Englishmen forbore to wonder why it had taken the President nearly three years to come to this rather obvious conclusion.'

The extent of American aid to the Allies after the United States entered the war is grossly underestimated—or even ignored—in every textbook. No mention is made of the rôle of the navy in the blockade of Germany, or its part in combating the U-Boats. One textbook only magnifies the crimes of its fellows when it reports: 'Thanks to the unceasing efforts of the Admiralty and the courageous determination of the Prime Minister, the losses declined steadily throughout the year and the rate of U-boat sinkings increased.' What reader could escape the impression that Britain, single-handed, triumphed over the submarine menace.

Authors show an equal reluctance to credit American land forces with playing any vital part in victory. Some, indeed, simply ignore the United States army altogether; others minimize its contribution by dating its participation in late 1918, rather than the spring of that year. Even when an author admits the presence of troops, he views their efforts with grudging tolerance. One concludes that 'A large American army was enlisted and trained, and did useful work in the last few months of the war, while the strength of the American fleet supplemented the power of the navy of Great Britain'. Another concedes that 'the Allies, now strengthened by American troops, continued their successes'. Text after text fails to describe the coming of the American soldiers, the campaigns in which they participated, and the flow of money and supplies across the Atlantic to provide the sinews of victory. No reader escapes the impression that Great Britain won the First World War almost single-handed, and that the American contribution was too late and too little to have much effect on the outcome.

The peace negotiations are handled with an equal lack of understanding and sympathy. Woodrow Wilson's sincere idealism, his hopes for a better world, his willingness to sacrifice his future and even his life for this ideal, are not revealed in a single textbook. Instead he appears as an irritating gadfly, standing in the way of a treaty that would give Germany its due. Lloyd George is the hero of the Versailles conference to English textbook authors, a judgment that astounds American readers. He is a man 'quick-witted and realistic, who tried to steer a middle course', and a leader with a 'natural and experienced agility of mind'. Wilson, in contrast, is 'unreasonable' or an 'idealist', with little understanding of the realities of European politics. That he is completely misunderstood by English textbook writers is shown by the recurring errors that mar their accounts: Wilson did not 'force' the conference to create a League of Nations but compromised on some of his Fourteen Points to gain its admission in the Versailles treaty; he did not dismiss Lansing before embarking on his speaking tour; he was not to blame for all the problems created in redrawing the map of Europe; he was not 'unaware of the trend of American opinion' while in France; he certainly should not have remained at home while the other Allied heads of state decided the fate of Germany; the American people had not 'already made up their minds to leave Europe to its own problems' when the Versailles conference was in session. Such errors are regrettable, but even worse is the failure of fully half the English textbooks to mention the League of Nations or ascribe to Wilson this sincere effort at bettering the world.

Accounts of Anglo-American relations during the First World War come close to open bias in the hands of most textbook writers in England and Wales. Not only are many of the authors hostile to Germany and Italy, but they scarcely conceal their resentment that the United States did not enter the war at its beginning. Worse still, they create the impression that Great Britain was solely responsible for victory, and that this victory would have come when and where it did without aid from other nations. Textbook authors in this instance have failed to divorce themselves from time as well as place. They mirror the prejudices of a people bruised by an agonizing war, and they reflect the attitudes of a war-burdened nation naturally resentful that sister nations did not come to its aid. They also show how lack of information, ignorance of modern scholarship, and inadequate space can cause bias as virulent as any excessive patriotism. A revision of these distortions is urgently necessary before the textbooks of England and Wales can free themselves of nationalistic prejudices.

VI
FINDINGS AND
RECOMMENDATIONS

THIS final chapter will first summarize the findings of the Committee on National Bias in Anglo-American Text-books, and then offer suggestions to future textbook writers which, if adopted, will lessen the distortions that now mar such works. It may be, too, that if teachers and publishers are also aware of the dangers they can be prevented as well as cured. The author is scarcely more at fault than the user and the publisher.

I. SUMMARY OF FINDINGS

As the first chapter of this report has already related, students of national bias isolate certain clearly recognizable forms of prejudice. These types guided the Committee in its analysis of the books used in the two nations. They can now be employed to suggest the degree and variety of bias encountered in today's most widely used schoolbooks.

(a) *Deliberate Falsification*

To accuse an author of *deliberate* falsification is to levy a charge that can but rarely be proved. Almost without exception writers believe that their utterances are valid and that their judgments comprise the untainted gospel. So far as this Committee is aware, no author of a secondary school textbook in England or the United States is liable to the charge of *intentionally* distorting history to favour one nation or the other. Nevertheless, some authors have strayed so far from objectivity, and always in the direction of national glorification, that they must be charged with falsification, even though this is not deliberate. A few instances may properly be cited.

In the United States these occur most frequently in Junior High school textbooks, where authors seem impelled to repeat discredited myths and enshrine outworn folktales. These writers, in some cases outstanding historians famed for their careful research, must know that they are dealing in untruths or half-truths, for they are competent scholars abreast of modern historical findings. Yet when such a writer entitles a chapter on the American Revolution 'The Colonies Unite to Resist British Oppression', he is either knuckling under pressure from a publisher to please superpatriotic groups or, more probably, has irresponsibly let someone else choose his title for him. Certainly he knows that the colonists were not victims of 'British oppression'. To use such a title when properly informed is to compound the crime.

Just as damaging to the cause of truth is the willingness of a few textbook writers to repeat disproven legends by using the evasive device of 'westerners believed' that Captain Hamilton of Detroit was a 'hair-buyer' who incited the Indians, or Ethan Allen was 'said to have shouted' his demands to the commander at Fort Ticonderoga. To repeat dubious, even false, statements under so flimsy a camouflage is to flirt with deliberate falsification. So is to reproduce, as does one textbook writer, a well-known picture of Samuel Adams pointing to the Massachusetts charter over a caption stating that he is 'pointing disdainfully to some new evidence of British despotism'. This is almost deliberate distortion, no less reprehensible than the out-and-out untruth of another writer that 'the British fired upon the minutemen'. Those who perpetuate untruths either deliberately or by some devious subterfuge must be charged with overt bias.

Almost as serious are the charges that can be levied against the authors of English textbooks for their one-sided accounts of Anglo-American relations during the First World War. The intent of these writers to produce objective history is demonstrated by their treatments of the American Revolution; as we have seen, their descriptions of that conflict sometimes lean so far in the direction of understanding the colonial position that they illustrate 'bias in reverse'. Paradoxically their sections on

93

the First World War show how little they have divorced themselves from contemporaneous emotions. The resentment generated by the refusal of the United States to enter a struggle that Britain believed necessary to preserve the western world still influences writers a generation and more later. How else can one explain the failure of textbook after textbook even to mention American aid to the Allies or the contributions of American military and naval forces to victory? Deliberate or subconscious, such distortions cloud the relations between the two countries.

(b) *Bias by Inertia*

Textbook authors who fail to incorporate the latest findings of historians, though not guilty of deliberate or subconscious bias, still distort the truth and damage international understanding. Many assumptions now disproved, and many interpretations now properly discarded, tended to glorify one nation at the expense of the other. So long as these outmoded viewpoints clutter the pages of textbooks, just so long will readers on both sides of the Atlantic gain an unfortunate impression of their neighbours.

Examples of 'bias by inertia' are legion. George III still survives in many American textbooks as a power-hungry monarch, buying votes and manipulating ministers to achieve absolutism; all this in contrast to the more recent scholarship which pictures that unfortunate monarch as a fairly competent and extremely conscientious king who sought to achieve certain administrative reforms amidst an impossible political situation. The British economic measures that fomented the American Revolution are today known to be necessary cogs in a chain of needed reforms that would allow a complex empire to function successfully, not punitive devices aimed at the thirteen colonies. By viewing the empire as a whole, as Britain's ministers did at that time, historians have gained a new perspective which alters their viewpoint on men and measures of the eighteenth century. They agree that the colonists would not have been content with taxation with or without representation, and that many 'grievances' were but propaganda fodder, if indeed voiced at all. Still the old cry of 'taxation without representation' rings from the textbook pages, and the list of 'oppressive'

acts yet provide material for charts summarizing the causes of
the revolt.

In discussing the War of 1812 American textbook authors,
particularly at the Junior High school level, show little awareness and less understanding of modern interpretations.
American entry into that struggle can be understood only by
appraising a variety of motivating forces, even though historians now agree that maritime factors were principally
responsible. This viewpoint has not penetrated many texts
which still stress 'western' causes and especially the need to
conquer Canada to quell Indian raids. To name this as the
sole or principal cause of the war, especially in the context
where it usually appears, is to plant in readers' minds the
impression that British agents were inciting Indians to attack
the borderlands.

The First World War also provides authors with many
opportunities to display their ignorance of recent interpretations, perhaps with some justification for this conflict has yet to
inspire the quantities of investigation lavished on the earlier
history of the United States. Yet to picture Great Britain, as do
some American authors, as one with France and Russia in the
network of alliances that upset the European balance of power,
or to suggest as do a few that Britain was armed to the teeth
and busily preparing for war for a generation before 1914, is to
distort the truth as now understood. Most textbook authors in
the United States display a woeful ignorance of the intricate
backgrounds of the First World War, and will never be able to
provide students with an objective account until they immerse
themselves more deeply in twentieth-century British and European history. English writers, as has been shown, are equally
innocent of knowledge of modern historical writing, especially
as applied to the War of 1812.

(c) *Unconscious Falsification*

Most of the bias apparent in both English and American
textbooks may be traced to a subconscious assumption of group
superiority on the part of the authors. To produce impartial
history, the writer must see with equal clarity all sides of the
story that he tells; a British textbook author must view the
American Revolution through the eyes of Samuel Adams and

George Washington as well as through the eyes of Grenville and George III. He should also view that Revolution as part of a larger revolutionary movement in the western world, one that was not without its impact on the internal history of Great Britain. Admittedly this is a difficult task, but it is not impossible. Intelligent reading of the sources and secondary works originating in all nations concerned, and constant awareness of the inherited prejudices that are part of every national culture, allows the writing of unbiased history, as some textbooks prove. Eternal vigilance is the price of history.

One elementary fault is the tendency of some textbook authors, especially in England and Wales, to associate the reader with his own culture by the use of such words as 'we' or 'our'. 'Our armies' and 'our people' are phrases that appear often in texts. This usage tends to allow the reader to associate with an exalted 'in group' that is sharply distinguished from all other 'out groups'. The result is a sense of superiority, with corresponding disdain for all who are not of the select circle. Translated into terms of nationalism, English schoolboys would effect a subconscious linkage with Britain's proud heritage; American schoolboys would feel as one with George Washington at Valley Forge or Andrew Jackson at New Orleans. National hostilities will inevitably result. Textbook writers would be better advised to write for all peoples rather than one.

Even writers who do not follow this unfortunate practice of using 'our' or 'we' sprinkle their books with repeated evidences of subconscious falsification. British textbooks dealing with the American Revolution mirror their authors' belief in English superiority when they avow that the regular army 'could be relied upon to beat the irregular levies of the rebels whenever they fought on anything like equal terms'. Authors show this faith even more when they ascribe Great Britain's defeat to the use of hired soldiers or suggest that backwoods fighting techniques were really not quite cricket. In both countries authors transmute defeats into moral victories or 'a miracle of strategy', as when George Washington accomplished his 'masterly retreat across the East River'.

The War of 1812 offers a similar opportunity to glorify one nation at the expense of the other, usually by devices of which the author is presumably not conscious. American writers invariably describe the burning of Washington by the British and almost as invariably make no mention of the American burning of York. Every textbook published in the United States dwells on the victory of the *Constitution* over the *Guerrière*; every textbook published in England and Wales recounts the triumph of the *Shannon* over the *Chesapeake*. American accounts stress the episodes that Americans like to remember: the few victories at sea, the Battle of the Thames, the Battle of Lake Erie, Andrew Jackson's victory at New Orleans. Much of the rest is forgotten; that is not part of the national folklore. Even what is stressed is seldom put in context, especially in relation to the Treaty of Ghent.

Similar distortions mar accounts of the First World War. Few American books acknowledge the achievement of the Allies in standing against the Central Powers for the three years before 1917; they instead leave the impression that the war began with the arrival of American troops. To some authors these soldiers turned the tide single-handed: 'their appearance in the battle line unquestionably heartened the Allies and seriously shook the morale of the Germans.' To others the battles during the war's final months were almost solely American victories. To English textbook writers the contribution of the United States was too negligible to deserve extended mention. Most disregard the aid provided the Allies before 1917, and most refuse to concede that American men and supplies had any appreciable effect on the outcome, although one admits that 'the Allies, now strengthened by American troops, continued their successes'. Authors in each nation apparently believe that their own men and materials outdid the Central Powers. This perversion of the truth illustrates the extent to which even reputable historians succumb to the pervasive belief in national superiority.

(d) *Bias by Omission*

Authors who omit materials that glorify another nation while including items favourable to their own perpetuate nationalistic bias no less than those who distort the evidence. The objective choice and inclusion of *all* facts and interpretations essential to understanding any episode is the only formula that can be followed in writing sound history free of the taint of nationalism. This is obvious, but those sins of omission that relate to the space allotted to any subject are more difficult to detect. Are English authors who dismiss the War of 1812 in a sentence or two guilty of national bias? Are American writers who begin the story of the First World War in 1917 without mentioning the burden borne by Great Britain in the prior three years victims of space limitations, or are they perpetrators of distorted history? Judgments on this form of bias are not easy to formulate.

Yet textbooks on both sides of the Atlantic provide a rich variety of examples of bias by omission, for the regularity with which authors 'forget' incidents unfavourable to their own nation precludes the possibility of memory failure. American writers who consistently make no mention of Washington's defeats while glorifying his victories can claim that they have told no untruths, but their total picture is untrue. The same can be said of those who fail to mention sectional divisions in the War of 1812, even to excluding mention of the Hartford Convention, or who retell the tale of successful military engagements while omitting the unsuccessful. Just as reprehensible is the unwillingness of some American textbook authors to include the few sentences needed to place certain incidents or policies in proper perspective. Thus writers bemoan the hiring of Hessians during the Revolution, but fail to say why they were employed or to make clear that this was a normal eighteenth-century practice. They dwell at length on British raids on American shipping before 1812, but omit to mention the even larger French toll of United States ships. Multiply these minor omissions, and the impression is created of actual falsification for nationalistic purposes.

In the very nature of their composition, textbooks used in England and Wales are more prone to the sin of omission than those published in the United States. Most are shorter than American texts, and all are forced to cover the immense time-span of British history from pre-Roman times to somewhere near the present. One of the ways in which they accomplish this is by paying shamefully little attention to Anglo-American relations. The American Revolution is always described, but the sentences allotted to the causes of the revolution are so few that inevitably the American case, the idealism and endurance of the people, the reasonableness of their arguments, is over-looked. The War of 1812 is virtually excluded from their pages, or dismissed in a sentence or two. No British student, reading these hurried accounts, could understand the effect of that war on the future of the United States. Similarly the First World War is usually treated in some depth by English authors, but most are so entranced by Great Britain's heroic stand that the contributions of the Allies are minimized, and those of the United States almost forgotten. These are grave errors of omission, and must be corrected before English textbooks contribute effectively to international understanding.

(e) *Bias in the Use of Language*

This expression of national bias is the semantic evidence of a subconscious feeling of group superiority present in nearly all textbook writers. None, obviously, seeks to glorify his own nation at the expense of another by the deliberate selection and proliferation of adjectives yet so inherent is the practice of self-praise by belittling neighbours or enemies, that nearly all authors succumb to the use of loaded words. Similarly, the all too common practice of phrasing questions or topical assignments in such terms as virtually to command a particular response is an equally effective device for encouraging partiality.

Semantic bias is particularly noticeable in textbook discussions of the American Revolution. To say that American militiamen in the Seven Years' War 'proved to British soldiers and officers that a colonist could fight as well and bravely as any man' will assuredly make the young American reader swell with national pride. To refer to the 'Intolerable Acts' rather than the 'Coercion Acts' is to mirror the colonial viewpoint, not that of the England of that day. To brand George III as a power-grasping monarch and Grenville as a 'narrow-minded' and 'obstinate and autocratic man', is to create an entirely false impression of the statesmen who sought to forge a workable empire system after 1763. Nor can American writers resist referring to the 'blunders' of British ministers, or the 'stupidity' and 'tyranny' of their measures.

Descriptions of battles similarly abound in phrases designed to stir patriotic blood: to American authors the patriots (a weighted word in itself) were notable for their 'deadly fire' or 'deadly accuracy', and for the 'brilliant campaigns' that 'struck terror' into the hearts of the enemy. Nor is prejudice on one side alone. English writers who refer to the Grenville policies as 'reasonable' without considering their defects, and to Britain's victories as 'brilliant' without weighing their significance, are also guilty of semantic distortion. These are not impartial words, and they are dangerous ones to employ in sober historical studies.

(f) *Bias through Cumulative Implication*

By a simple arrangement of cumulative facts, textbook authors can convey the impression that one nation has monopolized victories in war, or contributions to civilization in peace, when credit should really be shared with another, or many nations. One, for example, who simply lists inventions by his own countrymen without revealing that other countries have contributed to the inventive process is guilty of bias. Authors of texts used in the United States, and in England and Wales, have occasionally stooped to this form of distortion. They have also implied that either America or Britain won a disproportionate share of battles in the Revolution or War of 1812, or that one or the other achieved victory by its own herculean efforts without awarding credit to allies who bore a major share of the burdens.

Examples of these distortions abound. Virtually all textbooks, as has been shown, list the battles their nation has won but omit those that were lost. American accounts of the Revolutionary war rarely give proper credit to France in weighing the factors bringing victory; no one can understand that war without an overall appreciation of the world scene where French troops and French ships engaged the British on a dozen fronts. To ignore these, or to dwell only on the contributions of Lafayette and De Grasse, is to suggest by implication that American strength was far greater than it was. Similarly, Britain's preoccupation with Napoleon is seldom given proper attention by textbook writers in their descriptions of the War of 1812. An impartial history of that conflict should employ statistics showing the deployment of Great Britain's fighting men and ships throughout the world, and revealing the few forces available for the American theatre.

On the other hand, authors of texts in England and Wales have consistently refused the United States credit for its contribution to an Allied victory in 1918. Scarcely one details the vast flow of money and supplies across the Atlantic before America entered the war, and none deals adequately with American contributions to final victory. An author who writes that 'thanks to the unceasing efforts of the Admiralty and the courageous determination of the Prime Minister, the losses declined steadily throughout the year and the rate of U-boat sinkings increased' is closing his eyes to the rôle of the United States in a success that could have been achieved by neither nation alone. The repetition of half-truths, and the consistent monopolization of credit for the author's country, creates in the reader an impression of one invincible nation, forever right, forever triumphant, and forever superior to its neighbours. This is an image that is both false and dangerous in today's world.

That these forms of nationalistic bias are found in all textbooks used in the secondary schools of England and the United States is a matter of concern, but still understandable. Only recently have students become aware of the many subtle forms in which such prejudices can be manifested. Writers still think of bias as deliberate distortion, a practice seldom encountered in such liberal democracies as the United States and Great Britain. Until they realize that they must exert every effort to divorce themselves from the traditional beliefs of their own country, that they must exercise constant vigilance to view every episode from two or more sides, that they must be forever on the alert for nuances of expression, the textbook authors of America and England will be creators of national prejudices. They must also be more aware than in the past that history is not a dead subject, but one that changes as they write about it, changes because new knowledge becomes available and because every generation views the past through its own bifocals. Good intentions are not enough. New knowledge is not merely to be spread like frosting on a cake; it calls for a fresh cake.

2. SUGGESTIONS TO TEXTBOOK WRITERS AND PUBLISHERS

The writers of this report certainly do not propose to dictate or standardize the writing of history. The Committee considered, even outlined, 'model' treatments of the American Revolution, the War of 1812, and the First World War as a guide to future authors, but very quickly discarded that policy, not from caution, but because its members were fully aware that there is no one way to write a book, and that one man's truth is another man's bias. Every historian is a man of feeling and he is 'involved' the moment he puts pen to paper. The Committee's hope is only to make writers and publishers aware that nationalistic bias does exist in today's textbooks and to show them its varied and often subtle nature so that they may be on guard against it.

Authors who heed these lessons need not fear that they will be reduced to writing dull paragraphs, barren of anecdote or heroic episode, and deadening to the young. Unbiased history can be as exciting to the schoolboy as the most distorted fable, for human behaviour is so varied as to provide infinite examples for story-telling or speculation. The words that Ethan Allen probably uttered as he entered Fort Ticonderoga—'Come out you damned rats and surrender'—would certainly captivate today's youth more than his rumoured phrases on the Great Jehovah and the Continental Congress. Truthful history in textbooks does test the ingenuity of the writer, for he must ferret out his own examples rather than rely on discredited legends. But the reward is worthy of the effort, for the story that he tells will please his readers and contribute to their understanding of their own country as well as its neighbours.

While bias and untruth have no place in any textbook, the Committee recognizes that the problem of their elimination varies from country to country. The means necessary for the writing of objective history in the United States may vary extensively from those required in England and Wales. Hence the Committee's recommendations will be in two parts, one directed to American, the other to English, textbook writers.

(a) *Suggestions to American Textbook Writers*

Authors of texts used in the United States are seeking objectively, yet at the same time are the victims of subconscious prejudices that should be eradicated from their works.

Their principal need is a universal, or bi-national point of view. Instead of viewing past events exclusively from their own shores they should betake themselves across the sea, physically if possible, intellectually and emotionally at any rate. They must, to use a simple example, see the Declaration of Independence as it appeared not only to the colonists but as it looked to George III; they must view the Stamp Act through the eyes of George Grenville and the eyes of Samuel Adams. By immersing themselves in the writings of both participants in every event, they will see that event in new perspective.

This 'immersion' must go much further than the saccharine admission that 'of course there are two sides to every question'. It necessitates the effort to appreciate among many other things the world—the political, social, intellectual, even simply the geographical—world of 1763–1776, the effort to comprehend the background and environment of George III and Grenville, Samuel Adams and Jefferson, the attempt to discover *why* they did *what* they did, and how far their words and actions determined the actual course of events. Just because the man of 1965 cannot translate himself physically back to 1765 is no reason for refusing to put to himself some fairly elementary questions about 1765; indeed, what else is history for? He can at the very least inquire how much of a burden was the Stamp Act and on whom and in what ways, how did the presence of British soldiers actually threaten whose liberty, what would he have done about violence in the streets and smuggling, always remembering, as he considers the answers, as much as he can about the outlook and circumstances of the time on both sides of the Atlantic.

No less essential to American authors is eternal vigilance against weighted language. By their words shall ye know them. Tradition and training decree that every author has certain preconceptions about the familiar events of his nation's past, and that from his earliest historical experiences these events have come down to him under certain labels. Human psychology similarly decrees that each of us has a subconscious belief in the superiority of his own group, and with this a tendency to assume that his group really believes, for example, in liberty where others do not. These are mighty obstacles to be overcome if history is to be written objectively, and they can be surmounted only if every word is chosen carefully and every sentiment tested in the crucible of analysis. The author's own nation's victories cannot be 'brilliant' while those of the enemy are 'fortunate'. His country cannot win all 'major engagements' and lose all 'skirmishes'. Its statesmen must not be 'skilled' and 'generous' while their opponents are 'stupid' and 'grasping'. The nuances of language are as essential to impartial history as is objectivity in the weighing of evidence.

If they are to mirror the past accurately, textbook authors must also be aware that words constantly change their meaning. To freight the words of 1765 with the definitions of 1965 is to distort the image of events of that day. The writer of public documents during the Revolutionary era—whether living in London or Williamsburg—conveyed certain sentiments to his own generation that are not conveyed to today's generation by the same words. The phrases that he used have been changing their meaning ever since, and each subsequent generation has bequeathed a flavour that was not in the original. Textbook writers will do well to get back to the original documents, and will do even better to read them within the context of the time in which they were written.

Just as important is the need for awareness of the latest findings in historical research. Historians of past generations, unrestrained by the rules that govern modern investigation, were inclined to clutter their accounts with legends and folklore that were violently nationalistic as well as completely untrue. Scholars have laboured for years to cut away this crust of myth in order to get at the reality of the past. Just as long as textbook writers remain unaware of the nature and extent of these researches, the rejected beliefs of scholars will continue in their pages to fuel nationalistic sentiments. Authors who write today that George III was a tyrant, that the British fired the first shot at Lexington, that the War of 1812 was needed to stop British inspired Indian raids from Canada, are showing their unfamiliarity with present-day scholarship no less than their nationalistic bias.

In making this plea for familiarity with the latest scholarship, members of the Committee are fully and painfully aware of what it takes to keep abreast of today's flood of historical publications. They too are sometimes ambushed by ignorance in their own special fields let alone those outside; they too know the tremendous difficulty of simultaneously penetrating below the surface and at the same time remaining conscious of the broad vistas. But the textbook writer of today does have aids unknown a generation ago. Scholars, very good ones, are much alive to the need of making available not only the latest discoveries but also the latest interpretations. They contribute to first-rate popular magazines, *The American Heritage* and *History Today*; they write special pamphlets for the two national historical associations that are within the reach, physically and financially, of everyone; they produce excellent paperbacks, many of them assembling articles or brief special studies that emphasize the latest historical studies and theories; they are, we think, quicker to propound new interpretations in their classes. Even the sober and learned historical journals are increasingly aware that history is written to be read, and to be read it must be well written. To be well written it must have some style, and more than that it must seek some relevance with the present. The tools are there for the textbook writer to use; if he does not enjoy as well as profit from their use, he is in the wrong profession.

This broad program of reading recommended to the author certainly should not be confined to books about his own country written by his own countrymen. The writer of an American textbook wishing to present an impartial history of the Revolutionary era will be well advised to dig deeply into the works of British scholars that depict that event as viewed from London, or even those that impinge on the field in which they are writing. Thus no proper understanding of British policy is possible to a writer unfamiliar with the careful findings of the 'Namier' School on George III and the politics of the day. Conversely, any British author of a text should read what American historians have to say about Woodrow Wilson before venturing to describe the Versailles conference. These are formidable assignments, but the end of impartiality will justify any expenditure of time and thought.

Finally, American textbook writers should devote more thought to the balance of their accounts, in an effort to avoid the glaring omissions that reveal so much national bias. Every author, to be sure, composes within rigid space limitations; he must decide which of the hundreds of possible facts and inter-pretations he will include. Too often the choice has been for the colourful or the glamorous, and too seldom for the balanced array of information that would tell an understandable story. No writer should deliberately discard the interesting and en-ticing, but neither should he be forced to omit the essential. This means a constant exercise of the powers of selectivity, but it means also a recognition of the hard core of fact and inter-pretation necessary to make any event comprehensible and meaningful.

American textbook writers describing the Revolution should know that certain information is too important to be omitted: the nature of British party politics, the part played by France and Spain in the events leading to the war and the war itself, the principal parliamentary measures viewed as a part of the broader pattern of imperial reform, the internal divisions within the colonies that affected its outcome, the major military cam-paigns whether successes or failures, and the intricate series of negotiations that preceded the peace treaty. No history of the War of 1812 should omit an analysis of the many forces leading the United States into that conflict, a discussion of the world scene with its impact on Great Britain's military strategy, defeats and victories on land and sea, and the significance of the war and peace on American foreign policy and internal growth. Textbook chapters on the First World War should make clear that the Allies endured the burdens of war before the United States entered, that American military aid did not reach Europe in effective quantities until May, 1918, that casualties in men and goods were far greater for the Allies than for America, and that the Allied diplomats who wrote the peace treaty were practical realists rather than grasping seekers after territories. These suggestions are only a very few of the many that might be made. They are intended to suggest only that every author should weigh his facts as well as list them, and so make sure that the resulting combination will most accurately depict the event he is describing.

(b) *Suggestions for British Textbook Writers*

The suggestions to American textbook authors apply with no less force to writers in England and Wales. The books that they have produced in the past reveal the same forms of bias; they display a similar myopia by viewing the past through the eyes of Englishmen alone; they exhibit carelessness in the use of language; they fail to reveal evidences of familiarity with modern scholarship and especially that produced outside of Great Britain; and they lack the balance that alone achieves impartiality. In addition, authors of texts in England face still another problem peculiar to themselves.

This stems from the size of the books and the length of the story they have to tell. That they should be relatively brief is decreed by the limited schoolroom time allotted to instruction in history; that they should deal with a vast segment of the past is dictated by the lengthy span of British history. Understandably such books allot far less space to the American Revolution, the War of 1812, and the First World War than their American counterparts and, it may be said, far less than they properly might. Normally a textbook used in the secondary schools of England and Wales discusses the Revolution in a brief chapter, the War of 1812 in a few lines, and the First World War in a dozen or so pages. Clearly a major problem of English authors is the most meaningful use of a very limited amount of space.

The Committee suggests that the traditional space allotments in these books might well be revised to conform to the realities of the twentieth-century world. Clearly no author can reveal the full implications of the American Revolution, even for Britain let alone for the world, in a few pages, or of the War of 1812 in a sentence. Yet these are conflicts that should be understood by informed British citizens. For this reason the Committee proposes consideration of three suggestions: first, that English textbooks seek an approach that is less parochial and more world-minded; second, that Anglo-American relations be more fully emphasized; and, third, that phases of United States history be stressed when they impinge upon the history of Great Britain. These innovations seem worth consideration, even at the expense of certain aspects of England's internal history which have been traditionally stressed, especially where some of these aspects are expendable material.

Lest the Committee be charged with Anglo-American provincialism and duo-national bias, let it hasten to point out that such a reapportionment seems advisable in view of conditions in the modern world. Great Britain and the United States have for more than a century and a half lived side by side in peace, if not always in friendship. Today they personify the democratic values so essential to maintain in a world of clashing ideologies. These can be preserved only if the two nations continue to understand and respect each other. Understanding and respect can be engendered by historical studies, but historical studies can also change friendship into hatred, peace into friction and then repulsion, if they create biased impressions in the minds of their readers. Such bias is generated especially by over compressed accounts, for the more compact the historical treatment, the more evident the prejudices of the author. The Committee maintains that Anglo-American understanding in the future requires fuller textbook discussions of Anglo-American relations whether in war or in alliance.

This is not to suggest that a disproportionate amount of space be given to the American Revolution or the War of 1812; it is to propose that enough space be allotted to those and similar events to make them understandable to British youth. An expansion of the treatment of the War of 1812 seems especially desirable in view of the scant space currently allotted to that subject. For this reason, and to serve as an example of the greater understanding that can be achieved through the use of a relatively small amount of additional space, the Committee has prepared a few paragraphs that illustrate the complexity of that war and its impact on the subsequent development of the United States, as regards both its internal and external aspects:

The summer of 1812 brought significant events in the long war: Wellington's men entered Madrid, while Napoleon launched his legions against Russia. It also brought what Englishmen regarded as a tiresome minor complication, the War of 1812 against the United States. This was in the main a by-product of the European conflict. Britain, fighting for her life against Napoleon, interfered ruthlessly with American shipping. Desperately short of seamen, she impressed hundreds of men from merchant vessels on the plea that they were deserters from the Royal Navy. After issuing Orders in Council she stopped American ships on the high seas, searched them for contraband, and often confiscated their cargoes. These two practices, impressment and the exercise of the right of search, challenged American honour and seemed to make nonsense of the newly won independence of the United States. Moreover the blockade damaged the livelihood of many Americans, among them farmers and planters whose exports of crops to Europe were curtailed.

There were other causes of friction. On the British side many merchants saw the growth of American trade as a threat to British commercial supremacy. On the American there were politicians who wanted Canada and saw a splendid opportunity of conquering it while Britain was preoccupied with Napoleon; and there were many who believed that the British in Canada were aiding the Indians with weapons against American settlers. The United States declared war in June, 1812. Ironically, as a result of a serious trade depression which bankrupted many British manufacturers, the Orders-in-Council were withdrawn the same month, before news of the American decision reached England.

The war lasted two years and was a military stalemate. The Americans failed lamentably in their efforts to conquer Canada; the British failed equally lamentably to invade the United States from Canada. After the first abdication of Napoleon a force of Peninsular War veterans was sent to Chesapeake Bay; they raided Washington and burned its public buildings in retaliation for the American burning of York (now Toronto), but achieved nothing of military value. In the early stages of the war there were numerous single-ship battles at sea, most of which the Americans won; but the British navy gradually established a blockade of the American coast and the American coastal and carrying trade shrank to a tenth of their former extent. By 1814 neither country was fighting with much enthusiasm, and in December peace was signed in Ghent in Belgium. The diplomats reached agreement by ignoring the instructions from their governments and by saying nothing whatever in the treaty about such matters as freedom of the seas and impressment which had led to the war. A fortnight after its signature, and before the news had crossed the Atlantic, the Americans under Andrew Jackson shattered a force of British regulars which made a frontal attack on improvised fortifications at New Orleans.

The War of 1812 was neither a large-scale nor a distinguished conflict, but its consequences were great. For the British, to whom it was an insignificant affair, it meant the retention of

Canada, whose inhabitants, French and British alike, had shown themselves notably loyal during its course. For the Americans, by whom it has been called a 'second war for independence', it was far more important, notably in strengthening national self-confidence. They had lost no territory; they had acquired some patriotic memories and a national anthem.[1] The war stimulated American manufacturing and industry, and it encouraged the American people to turn their attention during the nineteenth century to the development of their own vast resources. Finally, the Treaty of Ghent was in some ways a remarkable turning-point in Anglo-American relations, not least because it set up joint commissions to settle the frontier between Canada and the United States—commissions whose work led eventually to some 4,000 miles of unfortified national boundaries.

In this manageable account, the salient facts are brought to the fore: the diversity of forces compelling the Americans to take up arms, the indecisive nature of the military phase, and the enduring significance of the conflict to the American people and government. Reading history such as this, English students will be better able to understand the evolution of the United States to its present position as a world power and the cordial relations between the two nations that have aided in this process.

Before concluding this report, the Committee begs leave to remind readers that although it has concentrated on three dramatic tissues of events, all the bias-types evident in the treatment of the American Revolution, the War of 1812, and the First World War can be found at other points in the textbooks of both countries. There have been other war eras productive of grave friction. The whole Civil War period at the conclusion of which, it has been said, Lee's veterans were ready to join Grant's against Great Britain, offer a fruitful field for the study of bias as it once offered a fertile field for bias itself.

At the same time it must be emphasized that although the piping times of war may heighten the problem, they do not monopolize it. The generations of peace have their stresses and strains no less than the years of war. The point is that an open crisis is not required to produce bias. If history textbooks are to

[1] The Star Spangled Banner was composed by Francis Scott Key, detained on a British ship during the attack on Baltimore in 1814.

further international amity instead of international anarchy their authors must always be alive to the bias implicit in omissions, weighted language, and outworn views. There is a place for national histories, of course, but not for nationalistic ones. No science, no political philosophy, no humanitarian reform, and no faults either are the possession, the peculiar possession, of one country.

That men have long recognized the dangers is clear from a warning composed over two and a quarter centuries ago by a writer who declared that there can be neither pleasure nor profit unless the historian is constantly on guard against the errors bred of passions. So many things, he said

> happen to bias our opinion . . . that the strongest resolutions of impartiality will prove insignificant unless we be carefully guarded against those temptations whereby men are not only daily surprised but, as it were, driven into errors and mistakes. Ignorance, education, religion and passion, and party-disputes are in a kind of confederacy to seduce mankind . . . Three things are required to complete the character of a [historian]— authority, skill, and integrity. Without authority, his sentence is void; without skill it is rash; and without integrity it is unjust.[1]

Today as one reads the textbooks in common use, particularly those in the United States, one cannot escape the feeling that much of the prejudice they exhibit stems from the ancient tendency of writers to *personalize* Anglo-American relations. As far back as the American Revolution itself, as indeed one might expect, men played off the 'base designs and evil machinations' of an 'old and contaminated' Britain against the 'hope and idealism' of a 'young and fresh' United States, the 'empty pomp and ceremony' of English aristocracy against American 'homespun democracy', 'hierarchy' against 'equality'. Today no responsible author puts the antithesis quite so simply, but the tradition is strong and many barely skirt it.

Having been made peculiarly conscious of this by its own studies of textbook bias, the Committee's ardent wish is that its specific recommendations will be interpreted more broadly than their own terms suggest. Its hope is that future textbook

[1] Hugh Tootel, *The Church History of England from the year 1500 to the year 1688, chiefly relating to Catholics* (Brussels, 1737), I, xi.

writers and publishers will not only recast their accounts of the American Revolution, the War of 1812, and the First World War to eliminate bias, but that they will apply the lessons of this report to all aspects of history. Its belief is that once authors are made aware of the prevalence of slanted language, feelings of group superiority, and the dangers of careless use of evidence they will write all history—whether of the American Revolution or an event in Anglo-German relations—more carefully, and with constant awareness of the nationalistic pitfalls that are strewn in the path of every author. The result would be a lessening of prejudice in the history textbooks of every land, assuring future generations a better training for life in a shrinking world.

INDEX

Academies, in United States, described, 20

Adams, John, defends British troops after Boston Massacre, 35, 49

Adams, Samuel, use of portrait of, 50, 93

Admiralty Courts, described in High school textbooks, 49

Aids for Teachers Series, recommended, 6–7

Allen, Ethan, legend of at Ft. Ticonderoga, 40, 45, 93, 102

American Heritage, recommended, 105

American Historical Association, as aid to teachers, 6–7

American Revolution, bias in descriptions of, 9, 93–6, 98–9, 100; causes of, 36–7; recommended treatment of, 106; treatment of in textbooks, 12–13, 29–66; treatment of in Junior High school textbooks, 30–44; treatment of in High school textbooks, 45–56; treatment of in English textbooks, 56–65

Aryan Supremacy, influence of myth of, 4, 8

Berlin Decree, in War of 1812, 70

Bias, forms of, 1–14; nature of 40; bias by cumulative implication, defined, 12–14, examples of, 100–1; bias by falsification, defined, 7–8, examples of 92–7; bias of inertia, defined, 5–7, examples of, 94–5, in treatment of American Revolution, 51–2, in treatment of War of 1812, 77, warnings

against, 104–5; bias in language, defined, 10–12, examples of 99–100, warnings against, 103–4; bias by omission, defined, 9–10, examples of, 97–9, in English textbooks, 57, 59–61, 77–80, 87; in Junior High school textbooks, 84; bias in reverse, in English textbooks, 57, 64–6; bias in treatment of American Revolution, 30–66; bias in treatment of War of 1812, 68–81; bias in treatment of World War I, 82–91

Boston Massacre treatment of in Junior High school textbooks, 34–5, 39; in High school textbooks, 48–9; in English textbooks, 62

Boston Port Act, in English textbooks, 62

Boston Tea Party, treatment of in Junior High school textbooks, 36; in High school textbooks, 49–50; in English textbooks, 62–3, 65

Brooklyn Heights, Battle of, treatment of in High school textbooks, 54

Bunker Hill, Battle of, treatment of in Junior High school textbooks, 40; in High school textbooks, 53; in English textbooks, 60, 63

Burgoyne, John, defeat described in Junior High school textbooks, 42, in High school textbooks, 54; in English textbooks, 63

Cadore Letter, in War of 1812, 70, 75

Index

Camden, Battle of, in American Revolution, 42

Canada, treatment of in textbooks, 10; in American Revolution, 41, 53; in War of 1812, 69–73, 76, 79; in World War I, 86

Central Powers, in World War I, 82–91

Chesapeake vs. *Guerrière*, treatment of in Junior High school textbooks, 70–1; in High school textbooks, 76

Chesapeake vs. *Shannon*, treatment of in Junior High school textbooks, 71; in High school textbooks, 76; in English textbooks, 78–9, 97

Civil War, American, bias in treatment of, 110

Clark, George Rogers, western campaigns of, 42, 55

Coercion Acts, see Intolerable Acts

Commercial Regulations, use of by British in American Revolution, discussed in Junior High school textbooks, 31–2, in High school textbooks, 45–52

Common Sense, as propaganda, 53–4

Concord, Battle of, described in Junior High school textbooks, 37–8; in High school textbooks, 51

Constitution vs. *Guerrière*, described in Junior High school textbooks 70–1; in English textbooks, 79; mentioned, 97

Cornwallis, General Charles, mentioned, 9; in southern campaigns of Revolution, 42; treatment of in High school textbooks, 54–5

Cowpens, Battle of, 54

Cumulative Implication, see Bias of cumulative implication

Currency Act, treatment of in High school textbooks, 45–6

Declaration of Independence, treatment of in Junior High school textbooks, 40–1; in High school textbooks, 53–4; in English textbooks, 60, 62–3

Declaratory Act, failure of textbooks to mention, 34

Direct Grant Schools, described, 17

East India Company, in American Revolution, 35–6

Education, English system described, 15–18; American system described, 18–28

Eleven Plus Examination, 17

England, textbooks used in, 3–14; educational system of, 16–18; teachers in, 20–4; purpose of historical study in, 26–7; in American Revolution, 29–66; in War of 1812, 67–80; in World War I, 81–91

Erskine Agreement, treatment of in High school textbooks, 76

Facts, distortion of, 2–4

Falsification, unconscious, defined, 7–8

First World War, see World War II

Ft. Crown Point, captured by British, 42

Ft. Ticonderoga, surrender of described, 40, 53, 93, 102; recapture of in Revolution, 42

France, aids colonists during Revolution, 53, 55, 56, 60–1, 63, 100; in War of 1812, 69, 74–5, 78; in World War I, 83–6, 87–8

French and Indian War, see Seven Years' War

Gage, General Thomas, quoted, 41

Gaspée Affair, treatment of in High school textbooks, 49

Gates, General Horatio, in American Revolution, 42

General Certificate of Education, 22–3

Index

Index

Index

Roosevelt, Franklin D., effect of national bias on, 1

Rule of 1756, treatment of in High school textbooks, 75

Russia, textbooks in, 4; bias in, 11; participation in World War I, 84

Saratoga, Battle of, mentioned, 9; treatment of in Junior High school textbooks, 42; in High school textbooks, 54; in English textbooks, 60, 63

Schools, of England and Wales, described, 16–18, 20–4; of United States, described, 18–23, 24–8

Secondary Modern Schools, described, 16–17

Service Centre for Teachers of History, operations of, 6

Seven Years' War, treatment of in Junior High school textbooks, 31; in High school textbooks, 45–7; in English textbooks, 65; distortions of in American textbooks, 99

Shannon, see *Chesapeake* vs. *Shannon*

Shelburne, Earl of, in Revolutionary peace negotiations, 55

Smuggling, extent of before Revolution, 47

Sons of Liberty, in Boston Tea Party, 36

Stamp Act, treatment of in Junior High school textbooks, 33–4; in High school textbooks, 47–8; in English textbooks, 62

'Star Spangled Banner', stress on in Junior High school textbooks, 68, 70

State Schools of England and Wales, described, 16–17

Submarine warfare, as cause of American entry into World War I, 85; treatment of in English textbooks, 88–9, 101

Sugar Act, treatment of in High school textbooks, 45–6

Suspending Act, mentioned, 34

Taxation, as issue in American Revolution, 57, 94–5; treatment of in Junior High school textbooks, 33–7; in High school textbooks, 45–52

Teaching History, recommended, 26

Tea Act, treatment of in Junior High school textbooks, 35–6; in High school textbooks, 49–50; in English textbooks, 62–3

Tecumseh, in War of 1812, 73

Textbooks, nature of bias in, 1–14; methods of selection, 21–3; use of in secondary schools, 23–5; contrasts between English and American, 56–8; treatment of American Revolution in, 29–66; treatment of War of 1812 in, 67–80; treatment of World War I in, 81–91; recommendations for improving, 102–12

Thames, Battle of, treatment of in Junior High school textbooks, 71; in English textbooks, 79; mentioned, 97

Tippecanoe, Battle of, in War of 1812, 73–4

Townshend Acts, treatment of in Junior High school textbooks, 34–5; in High school textbooks, 48; in English textbooks, 58, 65

Townshend, Charles, treatment of in Junior High school textbooks, 34–5; in High school textbooks, 48

Treaty of Paris, treatment of in Junior High school textbooks, 43; in High school textbooks, 55

Trenton, Battle of, in American Revolution, 54

Triple Entente, in World War I, 85

Unconscious Falsification, see Bias by unconscious falsification

United States, use of textbooks in, 3–14; educational system of, 18–20; purpose of historical studies

117